ONE WORLD MANY ISSUES

General Editor: Bernard Williams

Graham Langtree, Lyn Clarke, Mandy Kennick

Stanlishers) Ltd

Stanley Thornes (Publishers) Ltd

First published in 1997 by:
Stanley Thornes (Publishers) Ltd
Ellenborough House
Wellington Street
CHELTENHAM GL50 1YW
England

97 98 99 00 01 / 10 9 8 7 6 5 4 3 2 1

A catalogue record for this book is available from the British Library.

ISBN 0-7487-2981-X

Printed and bound in Italy by G. Canale & C. S.p. A. – Borgaro T.se – TURIN

Acknowledgements

With thanks to the following for permission to reproduce photographs and other material in this book:

ASAP: *Israel Talby* 101; Associated Press: *Eddie Adams* 119; Bridgeman Art Library, London: *National House, Petworth House, Sussex* 23; British Pregnancy Advisory Service: 57 (bottom); Camera Press: 113 (top), 126–7, *Frank Fishbeck* 125, *James Pickerell* 112 (bottom), 124 (both); Christian Aid: *Gideon Mendel* 86 (right); Colorific!: *Jim Pickerell* 82 (top); Corbis-Bettmann: 135; Daily Mail/Solo: 104; Department of Health: 50 (bottom), 72; Environmental Images: *Irene Lengui* 77 (centre), 86 (left); Glevum Windows: 44 (right); Greenpeace: 81 (logo), 89; The Guardian: 65; Helen House Hospice for Children, Oxford: 51 (bottom), 70–1; Hulton Getty: 29 (centre), 45 (second from bottom), 113 (bottom), 136 (both); The Kobal Collection: 91 (top), 104, 105; Life: 57 (top); Mary Evans Picture Library: 9, 83, 116, 122 (both); NCH Action for Children: 43; Network: *Homer Sykes* 133 (top); NSPCC: 5 (top), 12–13; PA News: 128; Panos Pictures: *Trygve Bolstad* 5 (bottom), 19, *Heidi Bradner* 78 (bottom), *Arabella Cecil* 115 (right), *J Hartley* 76 (centre), 80, *Jim Holmes* 16–17, 47, *Sean Sprague* 18, *Liba Taylor* 5 (centre), 16 (centre), *Penny Tweedie* 44 (left); Photofusion: *Bob Watkins* 30 (top); Redferns: *Kieran Doherty* 45 (bottom), 90 (bottom), 100; Rex Features: 20 (centre), 21 (centre and right), 45 (second from top), 112 (centre), 113 (centre), 118, 120 (bottom), 129, 133 (bottom), *Stuart Clarke* 112 (top), 115 (left), *J Sutton-Hibbert* 51 (top), 63; Science Photo Library: *Andrew McClenaghan* 76 (bottom), 82 (centre), *Petit Format/ Nestlé* 50 (top), 52; Still Pictures: *Mark Edwards* 77 (bottom), 82 (bottom), 87, 127, *Dylan Garcia* 77 (top), 84, *Paul Harrison* 28 (centre), 37 (top right), *John Maier* 35, *Brent Occlesham* 20 (left), *Thomas Raupach* 81, *Hartmut Schwarzbach* 91 (bottom), 106, *Onan-Unep* 115 (top); Copyright © United Feature Syndicate, Inc. Reproduced by permission: 115 (Peanuts cartoon); The Walking Camera: 28 (top), 30 (bottom), 94, 95, 98 (bottom); Bernard Williams: 29 (bottom), 37 (top and bottom left).

Every effort has been made to contact copyright holders and we apologise if any have been inadvertently overlooked.

Illustrated by Francis Bacon

Picture research by Simon Conti

Edited by Louise Woods

Contents

Introduction
One world

Unit aims

In today's world there are many religions. Although each religion is very different, they all share similarities and they all confront common problems. People ask many questions about meaning and value but do not necessarily find answers. The aims of this unit are to introduce you to some of the ways in which the major world religions attempt to answer such questions, recognising that there are some areas on which most of them agree, but that there are also important differences as well.

Key concepts

Everyone has beliefs of some kind: How do we know what to believe? How do we use evidence to decide what is true? When faced with these questions, the impression frequently given by the media is that the 'answers' are to be found exclusively within science. As human beings, however, there is another part to our nature – the spiritual aspect, which science cannot easily explain.

What is this unit about?

Christianity, Judaism and Islam present God as the creator of the universe. They believe that while the origin of the universe is due to God's actions, it is possible, at the same time, to accept that there may be physical explanations, often put forward by scientists, for how it happened.

This unit examines the ways in which religions weigh up the crucial and difficult questions raised by suffering and evil.

For many people, the pain and suffering seen on a daily basis throughout the course of history makes the idea of a loving God seem remote. We constantly witness acts of man-made evil; yet we often see individuals, throughout their lives and despite terrible experiences, acting with courage, sacrifice, understanding and compassion.

many questions

One of the greatest mysteries that the world religions have to face is 'Why do people suffer?' Every few months, news reaches us of some disaster and individual cases of suffering are witnessed on a daily basis. People can deliberately act in a very cruel way towards others, accidents can happen and cause unintentional suffering, and there are the devastating results of the force of nature.

Despite all the wonderful advances in science and medicine, death is still regarded as a mystery. The one certainty of life is the fact that we all die. Birth and death are the two things we all have in common. So what happens to us at death? What is the purpose of life if death is always threatening? These are probably the most difficult of all the questions that religious traditions set out to answer. In the overall view of things we are unimportant. A bleak (or perhaps realistic?) picture is that few of us will even be remembered a few years after our death. The major world religions offer a different scenario; one full of hope, of optimism.

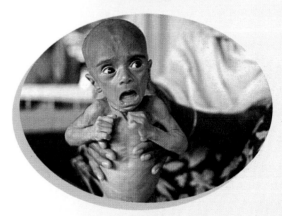

Big questions

In this unit, you will be thinking about important questions of meaning and the responses to them from believers in different religions.

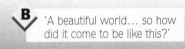

A What is 'spiritual'?

- exploring and valuing relationships
- exploring important questions
- our emotions, love, joy, anger, hurt
- valuing and caring for our environment
- **Spiritual**
- special moments in life, e.g. falling in love, encountering beauty and danger
- expressing feelings in art, music, drama and literature

Your targets in this unit are to:

- understand beliefs about good and evil in the world
- identify and explain the different types of suffering in the world
- consider and evaluate the arguments for and against the existence of God
- develop your knowledge and understanding of religious beliefs about the nature and character of God
- study beliefs about life and death
- express your own views and ideas about the questions in this unit clearly and in depth.

Life seems full of many questions, some of which appear to be easier to answer than others! It is clear that certain key questions are raised time and time again: *Who am I? What happens when I die? Is there a God? How did life begin?*

Such questions involve a great deal of reflective and critical thinking, but this approach leads us towards an important part of ourselves as human beings, namely the **spiritual** side of our nature. Many people believe that being human involves more than just 'flesh and blood'; it is our feelings and emotions that give us our identity as people. Diagram **A** above indicates some aspects of our spiritual nature. For some people the spiritual aspect of being human is more important than anything else.

B 'A beautiful world… so how did it come to be like this?'

any answers?

stop and think!

- **What do you understand by 'spiritual'?**
- **In your life, have you experienced any moments which you would describe as spiritual?**

C Statements about God

I want to know God's thoughts. The rest are details.
Albert Einstein

God's not dead. He's just working on a less ambitious project.
Anon

When God made man, she was having one of her "off" days.
Anon

God is dead. *Nietzsche*
Nietzsche is dead. *God*
Anon

God is really only another artist – he invented the giraffe, the elephant and the cat. He just goes on trying other things.
Pablo Picasso

If you talk to God, you are praying; if God talks to you, you have schizophrenia.
Thomas Szasz

D Statements about the purpose of life

I don't mind dying. I just don't want to be there when it happens.
Woody Allen

Life is like a sewer. What you get out of it depends on what you put into it.
Tom Lehrer

If a person hasn't discovered something they would die for, then they're not fit to live.
Martin Luther King

The person who regards their own life and that of their fellow creatures as meaningless is not merely unfortunate but almost disqualified from life.
Albert Einstein

I have come to give you life, life in all its fullness.
Jesus Christ

Life is like a tin of sardines – we're all looking for the key.
Alan Bennett

QUESTIONS

1 Read the statements in **C** and **D**. Discuss in pairs or small groups what you think each writer is trying to say.

2 What idea did you have about the word 'God'
  a when you were a small child?
  b last year?
  c now?

3 What are your views on life after death?

4 If life has a purpose, what do you think this purpose is?

5 Why do you think there is suffering in the world?

6 Explain why you think your views about God may have changed over the years.

The existence of God

Were there no other evidence at all, the thumb alone would convince me of God's existence.
Isaac Newton

God, why did you make the evidence for your existence so insufficient?
Bertrand Russell

B Sikh teaching

My true Guru [God] lives for ever and ever
No birth can envisage Him
No death can take Him away
He is Immortal Being and He is All Pervading.
Guru Ram Das

C Muslim teaching

All praise is due to Allah, who created the heavens and the earth and made the darkness and the light …
Qur'an surah 6:1

Both these statements in **A** are concerned with proof. Trying to prove something is not always as easy as it might seem. To the majority of people, certain kinds of proof are more acceptable than others. We have few problems with mathematical proofs, such as 'two plus two is four'. If a scientific experiment works every time, we know it is highly probable that it will work in the future. So, in the areas of mathematics and science, it appears that we can get precise answers to definite questions. With religious questions, however, it is far more difficult to present precise answers. One such question crops up time and time again: Can you prove that God exists?

In the past, some of our greatest thinkers have been concerned with this question. Clearly, it cannot be answered in a mathematical or scientific way, yet millions of people claim to know that God does exist. People who believe in God are called **theists**; people who do not believe in God are called **atheists**; and those who are unsure whether there is a God or not are called **agnostics**.

On the next page are listed some of the arguments people have made both for and against the existence of God. To understand the background to these arguments, it is important to understand first the Christian concept of God. The key ideas you need to remember are:

- God is all powerful – **omnipotent**
- God is all knowing – **omniscient**
- God is all loving
- God is the creator
- God is **infinite** and **eternal**
- God is ever-present.

stop and think!

'The existence of God boils down to a matter of faith. The various 'proofs' will reinforce an existing faith, but will fail to convince the unbeliever.

- Do any of the arguments set out on the next page rely on evidence more than faith?

- If you could have designed the world, what improvements would you have made?

A cartoon of Darwin, mocking his theory of evolution

The case for God

1 The 'design' argument
This view was developed by William Paley (1743–1805). Paley argued that if you found a watch on the ground (never having seen a watch before), a quick look at the watch would show a very complex piece of machinery, which had obviously been carefully put together. A watch could not exist by chance, but is obviously designed. The universe is far more complicated than a watch (for example, the human eye is far more complex than any human invention, such as the telescope, which can only *help* the eye). Therefore the universe must have been designed. The only possible designer of something as complex as the universe must be God, therefore God must exist.

2 The 'universe' argument (sometimes called the 'cosmological' argument)
This viewpoint was developed by Thomas Aquinas in the thirteenth century. Aquinas argued that it is impossible for something to come from nothing, therefore the universe must have been caused by something which existed before it. No matter how far you go back, there must be a cause that began everything. Something had to start the whole process. Aquinas went on to say that, with the universe, the first cause must be eternal – without beginning or end – otherwise it would have needed something to bring it into existence. The first cause, therefore, must be God.

3 The argument from 'experience'
Some people talk about God in terms of personal experience. They believe that they can know God personally by prayer. Within religion, believers sometimes talk about 'encountering God' through prayer and worship. Within the world of religion, some people believe that miracles are events which, because of their faith, demonstrate that God is alive and active.

4 The argument from 'morality'
Many people argue that all human beings have a sense of right and wrong and a **conscience** which helps them to decide what is the right thing to do. Our conscience is a sign of the existence of God, because human beings have been given the ability to make choices and can therefore choose good or evil.

5 The argument from 'people'
There are many people who have lived in an incredibly **sacrificial** way which stems from the faith they hold. In this century alone, Mother Teresa, Mohandas Gandhi and Martin Luther King have provided living examples of how a person's beliefs can affect the world in a positive, caring way.

It is clear that most of the major world religions believe that the demand: 'Prove to me that God exists' is unrealistic. The Creation stories found in most of the holy scriptures do not concern themselves with where God came from but simply state that God is. At the heart of all their teaching is the emphasis that the wonders of the world and the beauties of nature are not there by accident but rather by design. It is surprising to note that the attributes of God in all these faiths are surprisingly similar (**B** and **C**).

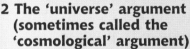

E Buddhist teaching

When I saw the great and wide disparity that existed in the world, I couldn't accept the creation.

Worlds of Faith, *by John Bowker, Ariel Books, 1983*

The case against God

1 The design faults
The world has got some major faults in its design and structure. The number of earthquakes, volcanoes, floods, droughts and diseases seriously calls into question the skill of a creator God. A much more likely explanation is that the universe is eternal in its own right and simply exists in a state of growth and change.

2 The Darwinian theory
Charles Darwin (1809–82) was the scientist responsible for the **theory of evolution**. He has, for some people, destroyed the argument of a designer God. His theory is that life has developed and evolved from very simple structures to reach the complex universe we now have. Through the process of natural selection, species have adapted to new and changing environmental conditions. Those species unable to adapt, such as the dinosaurs, have become extinct.

3 An 'unfair' God?
Some psychologists claim that religious 'experiences' are tricks of the mind, that if we want to really believe in something, then we will. With regard to miracles, even if some were 'true', then what kind of God is it that allows some people to be healed, but not others? This hardly seems a God who is fair and just.

4 The good conscience
Religion does not have a monopoly on **morality**! Many people who do not have any religious beliefs lead good lives and provide help and support for others. The existence of a conscience does not prove the existence of God. In fact it could be argued that religion has been responsible for more bloodshed and human suffering than any other human activity.

One world faith, Buddhism, strongly rejects a God who has created all things. It challenges any reconciliation between a creator God and a creation so full of suffering (**E**).

QUESTIONS

1 Of the arguments for and against the existence of God, which do you find the most convincing? Explain your answer.

2 Can you think of any other points either for or against?

9

In the beginning

- Is Genesis written as history, poetry, parable or another form of literature?

A

In the beginning, God created the heavens and the earth.

Genesis 1:1

B Christians believe that everything around them was made by God

For centuries, people have asked questions about the origin of the universe. Whilst many people feel that this question is one where science and religion are furthest apart, this is not necessarily true. There are some scientists who believe that when science finally finds the answers, there will be no place for religion, and there are some religious believers who dismiss scientific theories. However, throughout history, many people have explored scientific theories of origin, and have still believed that God is responsible for creation.

Christianity and Judaism

For Jews and Christians there is no question about who is responsible for creating the universe: God is (**A**).

Genesis tells us that in the beginning there was nothing but **chaos**. On the first day. God created light and dark, on the second, God made the sky and earth. On the third day, God divided the earth into land and water and then created all the plants that grow on the land and in the waters. God created the stars and planets, days and seasons on day four. On the fifth day, God created living creatures for the waters and those that would fly in the sky. On the sixth day, God made animals to live on the land and finally, he made Adam and Eve.

To make sense of any piece of writing, you must think about how it was written and who it was written for.

Christians believe that:

- the creation of the world and of life was not an accident. Everything was made by God for a purpose

- Human beings are alone in being given a special 'likeness' to God, and responsibility for God's creation.

Islam

Muslims believe that **Allah** created the universe. They also believe that whilst there are some similarities between the Genesis creation and the Qur'anic creation, there are also important fundamental differences (**C**).

Muslims argue that the Qur'an clearly shows that it is the word of Allah, and that Allah is the creator because it describes creation in scientific terms not known at the time it was written.

Islam teaches that:

- the existence of the universe and human beings is not accidental but the result of the will of Allah

- humanity is unique

- since Allah is the creator of all knowledge and 'true revelation is scientific', the Qur'an can withstand the challenges of science.

Sikhism

The Sikh religion, like Christianity, Judaism and Islam, teaches that God is the only eternal reality. All life forms, the planets and universes are deliberately created by God, are temporal (not everlasting) and will eventually disappear with only God remaining. God is present in all creation and within all human beings. The first words of the sacred writings, the Adi Granth, called 'The Mool Mantar' sums up the basic belief of Sikhism (**D**).

C Muslim teaching

It is He who created the night and the day, and the sun and the moon: All (the celestial bodies) swim along, each in its rounded course.

Qur'an surah 21:33

Do not the unbelievers see that the heavens and the earth were joined together (as one unit of creation) before we clove [tore] them asunder [apart]?

Qur'an surah 21:30

D Sikh teaching

There is one God, his name is truth eternal. He is creator of all things, the all pervading spirit. Fearless and without hatred, timeless and formless. Beyond birth and death...

The Mool Mantar

The 'Big Bang'

Some people say that the Big Bang theory disproves the religious versions of creation, but this must be looked at carefully.

a Firstly, it is very important to remember that this is still only a theory and not a fact or a truth. Scientists can only point to evidence supporting it.

b Secondly, scientists are not sure how accurate some of this theory is. Some of the mathematics involved suggest that there are planets which are older than the universe itself!

c Thirdly, this theory raises far more questions than it answers:

- What caused this explosion?

- How was so much created from the original two gases formed in the explosion?

- Is it just luck that the right two gases were formed, and that the explosion was just the right strength to promote the conditions necessary for life to start?

QUESTIONS

1 How do you think our world came into being?

2 If people believe in a creator God, how might this affect their attitude to the environment today?

3 Is it possible to believe in the Big Bang and evolution, and yet still believe in God?

Good and evi

stop and think!

'Perfect love casts out fear.'

'Evil occurs when good people do nothing.'

• How do you respond to these statements?

A This picture was drawn by a young girl who had been abused by a member of her family

The words good and evil are both powerful and important words. They are frequently used in the media. We speak of the 'evil' man who killed 16 children and their teacher at Dunblane in 1996, or the 'evils' of alcohol when someone is killed through drink-driving.

Human beings, both as individuals and groups, have been capable of enormous acts of wickedness and cruelty – you only have to think of the atrocious treatment of Jewish people in the Second World War – and yet human beings are also capable of acts of supreme love and sacrifice; giving up their lives for others, speaking boldly against **prejudice** and **discrimination**.

The media are usually far more interested in stories about evil than about good and it becomes easy to **stereotype** people as good or evil. Many films and television programmes are based on the battle between the forces of 'good' and the forces of 'evil'. Yet a lot of people would say that most human beings are a mixture of both good and evil.

The words good and evil raise an even deeper question, namely, 'What are human beings really like'? Like other important questions, religion has a lot to say about the human condition. How we see the role and purpose of humans is bound to influence our ideas of good and evil. In the sections on religious teachings (**B–G**), you will find a range of statements and teachings to help you think more about good and evil.

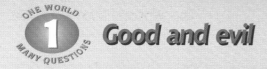

Good and evil

Christianity

Christians believe that human beings are born with **free will** – a choice of whether to do good or evil.

Because all human beings have done wrong, or broken God's rules, human beings need rescuing from their wrongdoing. They intend to do good, but give in to temptation (**B**).

For many Christians, evil occurs when human beings deliberately choose to ignore God.

Many Christians believe that a good person produces good deeds or 'fruits' whereas an evil person produces evil deeds. Evil is not also just action, but intent (**C**).

Islam

For Muslims, the source of evil is Shaytan (Satan) who seeks to destroy people by turning them away from Allah and causing them to do wrong. Muslims believe strongly that evil will always be punished, if not in this life, then certainly in the next. Those who do wrong must ask Allah for forgiveness and, as Allah is compassionate, those who are truly sorry will be forgiven (**D**).

 B Christian teaching

If we claim to be without sin, we deceive ourselves and the truth is not in us.

1 John 1:8

… The spirit is willing, but the body is weak.

Matthew 26:41

… When I want to do good, evil is right there with me.

Romans 7:21

For we are God's workmanship, created in Christ Jesus to do good works, which God prepared in advance for us to do.

Ephesians 2:10

C Christian teaching

The acts of sinful nature are obvious: sexual immorality, impurity and debauchery; idolatry and witchcraft; hatred, discord, jealousy, fits of rage, selfish ambition, dissensions [conflicts], factions and envy; drunkenness, orgies, and the like… those who live like this will not inherit the kingdom of God. But the fruit of the Spirit is love, joy, peace, patience, kindness, goodness, faithfulness, gentleness and self-control.

Galatians 5:19–23

 D Muslim teaching

For those things that are good remove those that are evil: Be that the word of remembrance to those who remember (their Lord).

Qur'an surah 11:114

And whoever does evil or acts unjustly to his soul, then asks forgiveness of Allah, he shall find Allah Forgiving, Merciful.

Qur'an surah 4:110

The (human) soul is certainly prone to evil, unless my Lord do bestow [grant] His mercy.

Qur'an surah 12:53

Nor can goodness and evil be equal. Repel (evil) with what is better.

Qur'an surah 41:34

Jewish teaching

> For hardship does not spring from the soil, nor does trouble sprout from the ground. Yet man is born to trouble as surely as sparks fly upward.
>
> *Job 5:6–7*

> For the Lord is good and his love endures for ever …
>
> *Psalm 100:5*

> … And what does the Lord require of you? To act justly and to love mercy and to walk humbly with your God.
>
> *Micah 6:8*

Judaism

Jewish teaching emphasises that people are free to choose between good and evil (**E**). If God ensured that the only actions we took were good, we would have little choice but to love him. Rejection of God and the performance of evil actions must remain a possibility, otherwise we would not have free will (**E**).

 Hindu teaching

> There are two orders of creation: one divine, the other demonic.
>
> *Bhagavad Gita*

> I know what is good but I am not inclined to do it; I also know what is bad but I do not refrain from doing it.
>
> *Mahabharata*

> No one who does good deeds will ever come to a bad end, either here or in the world to come. When such people die, they go to other realms where the righteous live.
>
> *Bhagavad Gita*

Hinduism

Hindus believe in natural and moral evil. The concept of Samsara, which is the cycle of birth, death and re-birth, is clearly seen as a natural evil. Human beings, however, perform acts of moral evil. The evil resulting from such actions is explained by the law of **karma**. The Hindu belief in reincarnation is also based on the law of karma in that the soul's next existence is governed by karma. The result of evil actions in a previous life can be improved by good actions (**F**).

 Buddhist teaching

> By oneself alone, evil is done; it is self-born, it is self-caused. Evil grinds the unwise as diamond grinds a hard gem.
>
> *Dhammapada 161*

> Many garlands can be made from a heap of flowers. Many good deeds should be done by one born a mortal.
>
> *Dhammapada 53*

> Not to do any evil, to cultivate good, to purify one's mind – this is the teaching of the Buddhas.
>
> *Dhammapada 183*

Buddhism

The Buddhist teachings concerning good and evil focus on the word **dukkha**, meaning the evil or diseased quality of life, which is something we all experience. Buddhists do not have to reconcile the concept of an all powerful God with the evils in the world. Evil and suffering are because of people's own selfish desires and actions. The Buddhist can try to improve the situation through good, purposeful actions (**G**).

QUESTIONS

1 What images come into your mind when you think about the words 'good' and 'evil'?

2 What do you think causes some human beings to act in ways we would describe as evil?

My life, my values, my experiences

In this part of the unit, we shall be thinking about the meaning and purpose in life, and what really matters to us as human beings.

Mark Twain (1835–1910), the American writer, once said that human beings are the only creatures that can blush and are the only ones that ever need to. Our feelings and emotions form an essential part of our humanity. So do our values. The way we regard people, and the concerns of our world say something about what is important to us.

What do these three pictures tell us about values? **A**

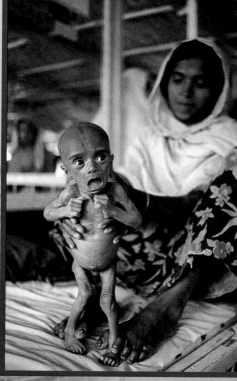

Decisions, decisions!

In our lives we constantly make decisions. Some are fairly easy and straightforward, others are very complicated. Look carefully at the statements in **B** about the factors which influence our decision making. Which ones are close to the way you make decisions about important issues?

All the major world religions have teachings which give guidance for their followers. Although many of the sacred writings were compiled hundreds of years ago, they are still regarded as crucial to the believer's way of life. All have similar themes running through them concerning people's experiences and the ways in which moral guidance can be applied in any age.

stop and think!

- What do you regard as the most important things in your life?
- Do you think that life has a purpose? If so, what is it?

Islam

The Muslim way of life focuses on the Ummah, the idea of all being members of one big family. Muslims are concerned about other Muslims throughout the world, no matter where they live. For guidance on all matters, Muslims refer to their holy book, the Qur'an, which is the word of Allah. The Qur'an is a full and detailed guide of how a person should live (**C**).

Sikhism

Likewise, Sikhs turn for advice to their holy book, the Adi Granth (sometimes known as the Guru Granth Sahib). Their society is committed to keeping three main commandments – nam japo (worship), kirt karo (work) and vand chako (charity). All Sikhs are instructed to live a useful, active and honest life, caring for others (**D**).

Buddhism

The goal of all Buddhist teaching is an attitude of mind and heart and an appreciation and care for all life (**E**).

 C Muslim teaching

My guidance shall come to you, and whoever follows my guidance, no fear shall be on them, neither shall they grieve.

Qur'an surah 2:38

 D Sikh teaching

Live amid the hurly burly of life, but remain alert. Do not covet your neighbour's possessions. Without being devoted to God's name we cannot attain inner peace or still our inner hunger... we must be moderate in everything.

Adi Granth 939

E Buddhist teaching

Let one's thoughts of boundless love pervade the whole world – above, below and across – without any obstruction, without hatred, without any enmity. Whether one stands, walks, sits or lies down, as long as one is awake, one should maintain this mindfulness. This, they say, is the sublime state in this life.

Metta Sutra

Making decisions

...ways weigh up each ...uation carefully before ...king my mind up.

...hink about the rights ...people involved when ...king a decision.

...ase my decision on ...v I feel about things.

...n always guided by ...y conscience in ...aking decisions.

...ake my decisions ...cording to the rules ...d laws which apply to ...e situation.

...y beliefs determine ...w I make decisions.

...hink about the ...nsequences and ...sults of the situation, ...en I decide what to do.

QUESTIONS

1 Read the following ideas about life. How many relate to your understanding of life?

Life is like a present... you never know what to expect.

Life is very hard and then you die.

Life is love, joy and valuing each other.

Life is a contrast of happiness and anger; peace and misery; love and hate.

Life is full of ups and downs.

You only get out of it what you put into it.

2 Read through the teachings in **C**, **D** and **E** above. Discuss them in pairs or small groups and try to establish whether there are any common teachings between them.

Suffering in

It is almost impossible to open a newspaper or watch the news on television without seeing some report of disaster or cruelty. The causes of suffering from such events are normally divided into two categories:

- **Natural evil** – when the normal patterns of nature are disrupted. Humans have little or no control over such events.

- **Moral evil** – suffering caused by the way people act towards each other and inflict pain by selfish or cruel actions.

A Evil and suffering

The twentieth century has probably witnessed more of man's inhumanity to man than any previous time. In world history, millions have died in wars – an evil on a vast scale. Then there is the untold suffering which happens behind closed doors. All this can be blamed upon mankind. We may ask why God allows us to do this to each other. For many people the responses from the world religions are clearly inadequate. Look at the ideas in **A**.

Some pain is good – it can be a warning.		
God works in mysterious ways.		
Suffering is a test of faith.	Suffering is a battle between good and evil.	If there was no evil in the world, there would be no good.
Suffering is the result of sin.	God is not all powerful.	Evil is an illusion.
Suffering is due to human thoughtlessness.	Suffering helps character formation.	God created the universe and then stood aside.

The aftermath of Hurricane 'Joan' in Nicaragua and flooding in Bangladesh, both in 1988 **B**

ur world

stop and think!

• Can human beings be blamed in any way at all for either of the disasters in B?

In the period 1970 to 1985, over 825 major natural disasters were recorded. To label a disaster as 'natural' often leads people to throw up their hands and declare that there is nothing they can do. Quite often, people are forced to live in situations where they are exposed to more frequent 'natural' hazards (**B**). Bangladesh, for example, has had 14 major floods this century. The most devastating of these occurred in 1988 when 46 per cent of the country was flooded, over 2,000 people died, and over 45 million were made homeless. Such incidents hold people back from belief: if there is a God, he does not make it easy for us.

Suffering and religion

Religions cannot be accused of ignoring the issue. The problem of suffering is particularly acute for the world religions such as Christianity, Judaism and Islam, which believe in a good, just and all powerful God. The evidence of evil and suffering appears to lead us to one of three conclusions:

• God does not exist

• God cannot do anything about suffering and evil, which means that God cannot be described as all powerful

• God does not mind that evil and suffering exists, which means that God is not good or these things are really good things in disguise.

Christianity

In the Christian **gospel**, the death of Jesus is followed by the **resurrection**, which gives hope to all who suffer. The suffering and death of Jesus is central to the Christian faith. The main religious symbol for Christians is the cross, a representation of death in its most hideous form.

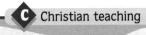

C Christian teaching

> Beware of turning to evil, which you seem to prefer to affliction [suffering]. God is exalted [glorious] in his power. Who is a teacher like him? Who has prescribed his ways for him [told him what to do], or said to him, 'You have done wrong.'?
>
> Job 36:21–3

stop and think!

• Is C a convincing argument or an easy way out for believers in an all powerful, all knowing and all loving God?

• If God is the creator, why didn't he create a perfect natural world?

• If God is the creator of humans, why didn't he create them so that they would always choose to do good?

• Can you think of any good which can come from suffering?

Suffering in our world

Buddhism

Buddhism, on the other hand, believes that pain and evil are related to ignorance. The **Buddha** taught a way of meditating, of living in order to overcome suffering, or 'dukkha'. These teachings are set out in the 'Four Noble Truths' (**D**). These are a summary of the Buddha's teachings from his first sermon and are based on the diagnosis that life is saturated with suffering.

The Buddha believed that there are three features which all things share. Firstly, nothing lasts and nothing remains unchanged. Secondly, that all life is affected by suffering. Finally, everything, including human beings, is subject to continual change and must eventually disintegrate. According to the Buddha, however, there is only one eternal, unchanging reality and that is **nirvana**: the ultimate aim of the Buddhist way. The connection between ordinary life and nirvana is also found in the Four Noble Truths.

In addition to the Four Noble Truths, and as an extension to the three features set out above, Buddhists are urged to follow the Eightfold Path (**E**).

Human existence is said to be unsatisfactory and full of suffering	Dukkha arises because of our desires
Dukkha can cease if we put an end to our craving	The way to overcome dukkha is to set out in the Eightfold Path

D The Four Noble Truths

E The Eightfold Path

stop and think!

- In Buddhist thought, suffering means always wanting something else. Is it possible to reach a point where we have everything we want?
- Does the Eightfold Path lead us to a way beyond these desires?

I After the Gulf War, some of the destroyed oil wells in Kuwait spilled petroleum on the desert, forming rivers, ponds, and lakes of crude oil. While most of the wells caught fire, some just gushed oil for months before they were stopped.

J Before a Liverpool – Nottingham Forest football match in 1989, 95 fans were crushed to death against fences surrounding the field, as gatecrashers surged into Hillsborough Stadium in Sheffield

K Drought and famine in Burkina Faso, one of the poorest countries in the world

The world religions make it clear that suffering and evil are quite distinct. Evil always results in suffering, but suffering is an important part of life which is to be avoided if possible, but which is not necessarily evil.

The passenger ferry, the *Herald of Free Enterprise* capsized in 1987 just outside Zeebrugge on the Belgian coast, with a loss of more than 180 passengers (**L**), and an earthquake in Kobe, Japan, in January 1995 resulted in the deaths of nearly 5,500 people (**M**). Both disasters caused great suffering but cannot be described as 'evil'.

A lot of suffering can be seen as our fault, but there is a lot beyond our control. This fact makes some people give up their faith completely. Either God does not want to help us or cannot help us, or there is no God.

Central to the beliefs of most of the world religions is the view that humans have free will, which can result in good or evil deeds. Sikhs, for example, believe that it is up to the individual to choose between good and evil (**F**). Islam believes that life is a series of tests (**G**), whereas Jewish teaching emphasises that suffering can be a test, a punishment or even a means to draw someone closer to God (**H**).

G Muslim teaching

Be sure we shall test you with something of fear and hunger, some loss in goods or lives… but give glad tidings to those who patiently persevere – who say, when afflicted with calamity [misfortune]: 'To Allah we belong, and to him is our return.'

Qur'an surah 2:155–6

H Jewish teaching

… When their… hearts are humbled and they pay for their sin, I will remember my covenant [agreement]… and I will remember the land… They will pay for their sins because they rejected my laws and abhorred [scorned] my decrees.

Leviticus 26:41–3

F Sikh teaching

Both poison and nectar are made by the Creator; both fruits grow on the tree of this world. Everything is in the Creator's hands. We are given to eat as much of them as it pleases God to give us.

Adi Granth 1172–9

stop and think!

- To what extent might the Jewish, Muslim and Sikh teachings help believers to cope with suffering?

QUESTIONS

Study photos **I** to **M**. Is it possible to say who or what was reponsible for the suffering in each photo? Copy and complete the following table to explain your answers.

Photo	Natural or moral evil?	Responsibility
I		
J		
K		
L		
M		

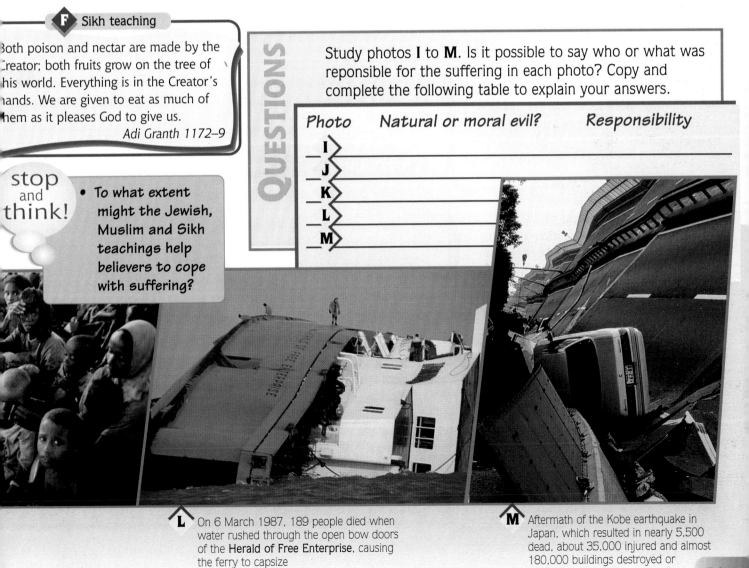

L On 6 March 1987, 189 people died when water rushed through the open bow doors of the **Herald of Free Enterprise**, causing the ferry to capsize

M Aftermath of the Kobe earthquake in Japan, which resulted in nearly 5,500 dead, about 35,000 injured and almost 180,000 buildings destroyed or damaged

ONE WORLD
1
MANY QUESTIONS

Life after death

A Phrases people use when speaking about death

> **passed on**

> **kicked the bucket**

> **croaked**

B

> We believe in life before death.
> *Christian Aid*

> He gives life and causes death, and to him you shall be brought back.
> *Qur'an surah 10:56*

C Christian teaching

> Where, O death, is your victory? Where, O death, is your sting? The sting of death is sin, and the power of sin is the law. But thanks be to God! He gives us the victory through our Lord Jesus Christ.
> *1 Corinthians 15:55–57*

> ... I am the resurrection and the life. He who believes in me will live, even though he dies; and whoever lives and believes in me will never die ...
> *John 11:25–26*

D Christian teaching

> ... each person was judged according to what he had done... If anyone's name was not found written in the book of life, he was thrown into the lake of fire ... the cowardly, the unbelieving, the vile, the murderers... and all liars – their place will be in the fiery lake of burning sulphur. This is the second death.
> *Revelation 20:13,15; 21:8*

Of the many questions human beings have asked, perhaps the most intriguing is 'What happens when I die?' (**B**). The three most common beliefs about what happens after death are:

● your body rots into the ground and that is the end, or

● you go to heaven or hell, or

● you are reborn.

Because we have no control over death, it is a question which continually puzzles us. Death evokes a whole range of powerful feelings and emotions. Fear, anxiety, shock, pain, loss, hurt, anger, relief (when someone we care about has suffered for a long time in pain) are all words associated with death. However, for some people, death is seen as a form of release, an end to suffering or simply a doorway to another life. Other people, whose lives have been fulfilling, appear to approach death with a sense of calm and peace.

Christianity

Christians believe that because Jesus conquered death through the resurrection, death is not something to be afraid of. The Apostle's Creed (an important statement of key Christian beliefs) states that 'we believe in the resurrection of the body and the life everlasting'.

Jesus told his followers that 'In my father's house are many rooms and I am going to prepare a place for you'. Most Christians, therefore, believe that there is life after death; that while the body decays, the soul will live on. In John's Gospel, Jesus also refers to life after death (**C**).

Most Christians believe that when people die, they will have to account for what they have done in their lives. For a long time, Christians believed that a life lived according to God's rules would be rewarded with a place in heaven, whereas a life which has ignored God will result in punishment in hell. The Bible describes hell in vivid and powerful language (**D**).

Not all Christians believe in a literal heaven or hell; some Christians find it difficult to accept the idea of a loving God cruelly punishing people. For some Christians, hell is regarded as the absence of God and all the characteristics of God such as love, joy and peace. The funeral service within the Christian tradition expresses a clear belief that death is not the end, but a gateway to a new life.

How does this picture show the idea of judgement?

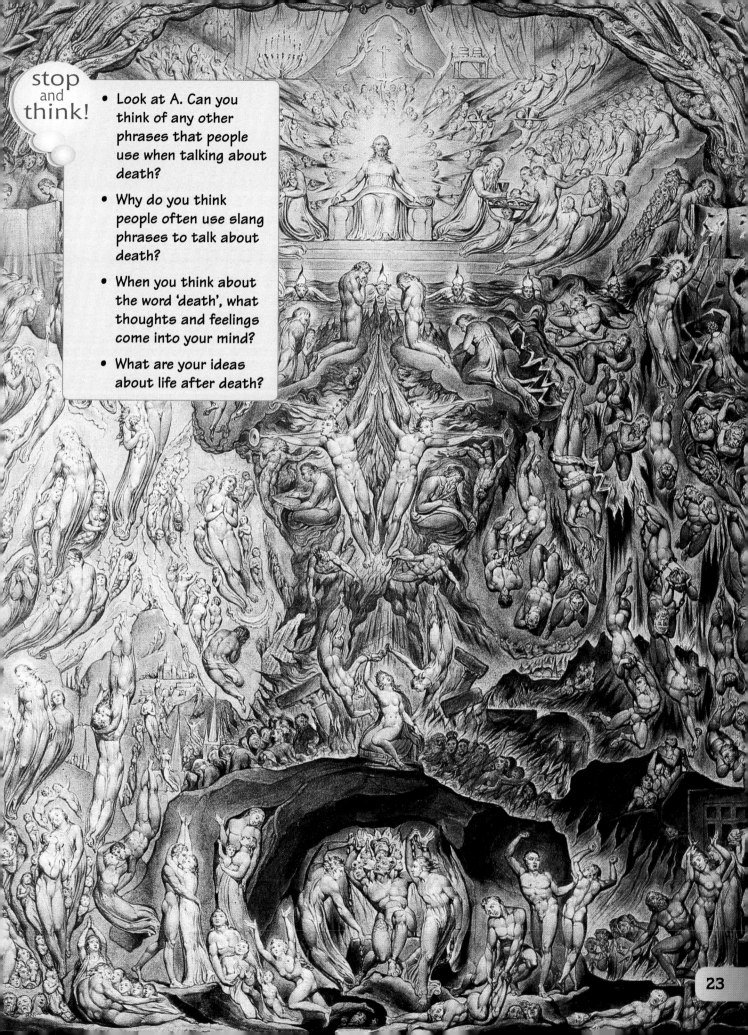

- Look at A. Can you think of any other phrases that people use when talking about death?

- Why do you think people often use slang phrases to talk about death?

- When you think about the word 'death', what thoughts and feelings come into your mind?

- What are your ideas about life after death?

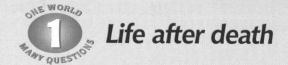

Life after death

Most religions believe in some kind of life after death and this is usually connected with how people have lived on earth and whether they have followed their faith.

stop and think!

- What ideas come into your head when you think of heaven or hell?

Islam

Muslims believe that all humans will be judged by God according to how they have followed the Qur'an and the **'Shari'ah'** (**F**). The Shari'ah is the law that decides what behaviour is right (halal) and wrong (haram). People who 'pass' the final test will be with God in heaven for eternity, but hell waits for those who 'fail' the judgement test.

Muslims believe that Allah is compassionate and, therefore, will forgive faithful Muslims who have lived as closely as they can to the message of the Qur'an At the funeral ceremony, Muslims ask Allah's forgiveness for the dead person's wrongdoings. Words from the Qur'an are spoken at the funeral ceremony. Muslims are never cremated because of the belief that Allah will raise their bodies from the graves on the Last Day.

F Muslim teaching

... the record (of deeds) will be placed open; The unbelievers will be led to hell in crowd: until, when they arrive there, its gates will be opened and its keepers will say, 'Did not messengers come to you from among yourselves, rehearsing to you the signs of your Lord, and warning you of the meeting of this day of yours?'... And those who feared their Lord will be led to the Garden in crowds: until behold, they arrive there; its gates shall be opened; and its keepers will say: 'Peace be upon you!'

Qur'an surah 39:71, 73

To Allah we belong, and to Him is our return.

Qur'an surah 2:156

G Jewish teaching

I believe with perfect faith that there will be a resurrection of the dead at a time when it will please the Creator blessed by his name and exalted by the remembrance of him for ever and ever.

The 'Thirteen Principles of Faith' number 13

Judaism

The central **Orthodox** Jewish belief on life after death is similar to that in Christianity and Islam (**G**).

Burials in Judaism are usually very simple as a reminder that people are born into the world equal, and should leave it the same way.

A Jewish burial is followed by a week of **mourning** called the 'Shiva'. Friends bring food so there is no need to cook and all the focus is on the emotions of mourning. A special Jewish prayer, the 'Kaddish' is said (this prayer is repeated every year on the anniversary of the death of a parent by the children). The Kaddish prayer does not mention the dead person by name, but asks God for peace.

Reform Jews are more likely to focus on the life on earth rather than the after-life. The Reform Prayer Book, for example, contains the words: 'what can we know of death, we who cannot understand life?'.

H Jewish teaching

Blessed, praised and glorified be the Name of the Holy One, blessed be He. He who makes peace in His high places, may he make peace for us and for all Israel and say Amen.

The Kaddish

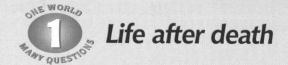

Hinduism

The central Hindu belief is in **reincarnation**. The soul (Atman) is immortal but is continually reborn. Hinduism sees life like a journey on which we take sixteen important steps (known as 'samskars'). Cremation is the sixteenth samskar.

The law of Karma (action) means that how you live your life affects how your soul will be reborn in your next incarnation. The aim of life for Hindus is to reach Moksha (liberation from the cycle of life and death) (**I**).

In Moksha, Hindus become one with Brahman (the ultimate reality) and the continuous cycle of birth, death and rebirth is over. Unlike Christianity and Islam, Hinduism does not speak of an eternal punishment.

 I Hindu teaching

As a man abandons his worn out clothes and acquires new ones, so when the body is worn out, a new one is acquired by the self, who lives within: The self cannot be pierced or burned, made wet or dry. It is everlasting and infinite, standing on the motionless foundation of eternity. It is beyond all thought, all change. Knowing this you should not grieve.

Bhagavad Gita 2:19–25

Those, however, who have no understanding,
who are unmindful and always impure,
do not reach the goal but go on to reincarnation.
Those, however, who have understanding,
who are mindful and always pure,
reach the goal from which they are not born again.

Katha Upanishad 3:7–8

QUESTIONS

1 'Death is both our deepest mystery and our greatest taboo.'

  a What is meant by the word 'taboo'?

  b Can you think of other 'taboos' in your life?

2 All religions put forward explanations of death and what lies beyond. There appear to be many areas of agreement but there are also crucial differences. Look at the various teachings and try to identify these similarities and differences.

1 Briefly describe what the following words mean:

    a Dukkha

    b Karma

    c Samsara

    d Ummah

    e Omnipotent

    f Resurrection

    g Reincarnation

    h Moksha

2 State what is meant by the following:

    a the Eightfold Path

    b the Four Noble Truths

    c theism, atheism and agnosticism

3 'The only way of proving God's existence is by experiencing God.' Do you agree or disagree with this statement?

 4 'The world is designed, so there must be a designer. The designer must be God.' Do you agree? Give reasons for your answer, showing that you have considered other points of view.

5 Apart from evil and suffering, what are the main arguments against the existence of God?

 6 Within one of the religions you have studied, how would a believer describe the character of God?

 7 'If God were good, he would wish to make his creatures perfectly happy, and if God were almighty, he would be able to do what he wished. But the creatures are not happy. Therefore God lacks either goodness or power, or both.' (**The Problem of Pain** by C S Lewis)

Explain the dilemma that suffering can cause the person who has a strong belief in God.

8 When faced with evil and suffering, why is a Buddhist less troubled than a Christian?

9 Explain what actions you would regard as evil, and why.

10 Explain the response of one religion you have studied to the problem of evil and suffering.

11

Cancer victim buried today

RAIL DISASTER – 21 KILLED

Baby abandoned by drug addict mother

Earthquake destroys four villages

Bombing campaign growing

All the above are recent newspaper headlines. Describe the different kinds of suffering in each.

12 'Suffering can create a better and stronger person.' How far would you agree with this statement?

13 Using information from the religions you have studied, describe what life after death might be like.

14 How might a person's belief in life after death affect their attitudes, behaviour and relationships in this life?

15 Explain why the resurrection is so important to Christians today.

16 Explain the beliefs of one religion other than Christanity about life after death.

Introduction One world

Unit aims

The strong emphasis in all religions is to regard the family as the base from where you learn everything in life. All moral standards, charity and love start from the family. The main aim of this unit is to give you the opportunity to explore the significance of good relationships in life and the challenges people face in their relationships with others. It is important to identify the responsibilities we have and understand the moral and religious principles which influence attitudes and behaviour.

Key concepts

Aspects such as family, marriage and human sexuality are not always easy to understand in our society. One advantage of holding a religious faith is that, normally, very clear guidelines are set out on the ways in which a person should behave. As we shall see, it is not always easy to commit ourselves to putting belief into action, especially when every day we receive many 'mixed messages' about relationships from the media, friends, school and home.

What is this unit about?

The word 'family' can be interpreted in many different ways. To some, 'family' refers to those immediate relatives with whom you live, but it can also include all those people related to you either by birth or marriage. You will find that, for all religious traditions, family life is of utmost importance. This unit illustrates that the exact form it takes sometimes varies, but in almost every society it is evident and seems to suit the needs of most people.

This unit is also concerned with the millions of children who suffer because of the actions of adults. Many are abused, sent out to work at a very young age or are denied their rights because of disasters, wars, poverty and disease. The world religions are increasingly uneasy because the basic needs of millions of children are largely being ignored. Their teachings are quite clear: all children must be protected and their rights must be upheld.

one family?

The word 'love' is frequently used to describe a range of experiences but it is important to recognise there is a spiritual as well as a physical dimension to its use. It is this former theme that can be seen in the teachings of all the world faiths. Alongside the virtue of love is the essential concept of forgiveness.

Although it might take different forms, marriage in every society is always regarded as a special event. Marriage is a relationship based on love between a man and a woman: a commitment which is usually freely given. To some, however, marriage is no longer seen as necessary for the raising of children or social stability and divorce appears to be steadily increasing.

This unit looks at what is 'normal'. A glance at any newsagent's shelf confirms that to be 'normal' you must be sexually active. This message is reinforced on television, on the cinema screens, and by means of the advertising that we are confronted with on a daily basis. In this atmosphere of 'normality' it is often suggested that individuals holding to the teachings of any religious faith can appear to be rather 'old fashioned'.

Family

What differences do you notice between these two family portraits?

life

Photograph **A** is a family with grandparents, parents and children, whereas photograph **B** depicts just parents and children. We call the former an extended family, the latter a nuclear family. In the last few decades, two additional terms have come into use: 'reconstituted' (step) and 'one-parent' families.

stop and think!

- What do you think are the advantages of an extended family?
- What could be some of the disadvantages of an extended family?

Nuclear

This is the traditional family so frequently depicted in the media today: husband, wife and children living as one unit.

Extended

The extended family consists of several generations possibly living in the same household with other relatives living nearby. This is still very common in some societies, but not so much in Britain.

Reconstituted (step)

When a marriage ends, children often find themselves being brought up in a new situation where at least one parent has re-married.

One-parent

Due to the increasing number of divorces, many children find themselves being brought up by one parent alone, usually the mother.

Some couples decide to live together (cohabit) without getting married. Such relationships can be long lasting and very stable. In English law, these are known as 'common law' marriages. Single people, who can be widowed, divorced or unmarried, do not live within a family community but may still be members of a family, normally an extended one.

2 Family life

It is clear that over the last fifty years our concept of the 'family' has changed a great deal. It is not the size of the family that is of importance but rather what it does (**C**).

The family unit is still seen as having a crucial function. In some societies and religious traditions the structure has not radically altered for centuries, but in the West there has been a huge increase in family break-ups. Some of the world religions have had to accommodate this within their central beliefs.

C The role of the family

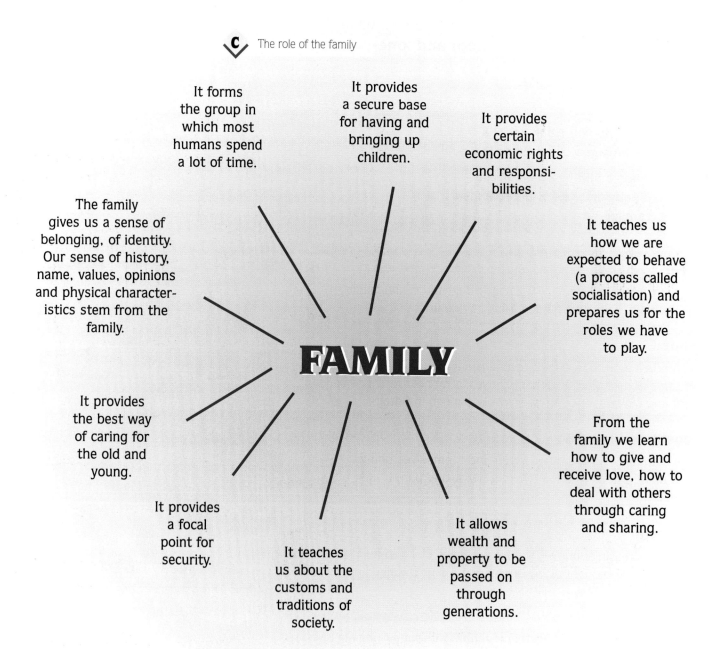

It forms the group in which most humans spend a lot of time.

It provides a secure base for having and bringing up children.

It provides certain economic rights and responsibilities.

The family gives us a sense of belonging, of identity. Our sense of history, name, values, opinions and physical characteristics stem from the family.

It teaches us how we are expected to behave (a process called socialisation) and prepares us for the roles we have to play.

FAMILY

It provides the best way of caring for the old and young.

From the family we learn how to give and receive love, how to deal with others through caring and sharing.

It provides a focal point for security.

It teaches us about the customs and traditions of society.

It allows wealth and property to be passed on through generations.

Many families encounter problems which need to be faced and overcome. Some of these are set out in **D**.

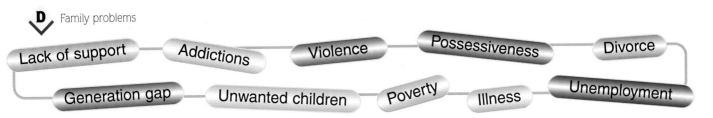

D Family problems

Lack of support — Addictions — Violence — Possessiveness — Divorce

Generation gap — Unwanted children — Poverty — Illness — Unemployment

All the world religions appear to believe that there is a need for mutual respect and tolerance in the family and that there are three main elements necessary for bringing up a family:

love   freedom   discipline

Some views of three religious faiths are given in **E**, **F** and **G** below.

E Christian teaching

Children, obey your parents in the Lord, for this is right. 'Honour your father and mother'… Fathers, do not exasperate your children; instead, bring them up in the training and instruction of the Lord.

Ephesians 6:1–2,4

F Jewish teaching

Listen to your father, who gave you life, and do not despise your mother when she is old. The father of a righteous man has great joy; he who has a wise son delights in him. May your father and mother be glad; may she who gave you birth rejoice!

Proverbs 23:22,24–25

G Muslim teaching

And We have enjoined [commanded] man in respect of his parents – his mother bears him… and his weaning takes two years – Be grateful to Me and to both your parents; to Me is the eventual coming.

Qur'an surah 31:14

Do not ask me to be a witness to injustice. Your children have the right to receive equal treatment as you have the right that they should honour you.

Hadith

QUESTIONS

1 Define what you understand by the word 'family'.

2 What is the ideal family, in your opinion?

3 Can you think of any advantages and disadvantages of being brought up in a one-parent family?

4 Many people believe that the 'family' is the foundation of society and it is as important today as it has ever been. What do you think? Give reasons for your answers.

5 Look at **D**. Can you think of any other family problems?

6 What issues do you think cause the most arguments in a family?

7 Do you think it is possible to discipline someone and, at the same time, love them and give them freedom?

8 Why are love, freedom and discipline all seen as so necessary in bringing up a family?

ONE WORLD
2
ONE FAMILY?

The rights of the child

 A Christian teaching

People were bringing little children to Jesus to have him touch them, but the disciples rebuked them. When Jesus saw this, he was indignant. He said to them, 'Let the little children come to me, and do not hinder them, for the kingdom of God belongs to such as these. I tell you the truth, anyone who will not receive the kingdom of God like a little child will never enter it.' And he took the children in his arms, put his hands on them and blessed them.

Mark 10:13–16

Children, obey your parents in everything, for this pleases the Lord. Fathers, do not embitter your children, or they will become discouraged.

Colossians 3:20–1

 B Muslim teaching

May his nose be rubbed in dust who found his parents approaching old age and lost his right to enter Paradise because he did not look after them.

Hadith

Your children are not your children.
They are the sons and daughters of Life's longing for itself.
They came through you but not from you,
And though they are with you yet they belong not to you.
You may give them your love but not your thoughts,
For they have their own thoughts.
You may house their bodies but not their souls,
For their souls dwell in the house of tomorrow, which you cannot visit, not even in your dreams.

Kahlil Gibran, The Prophet, Mandarin Paperback, 1994

With regard to children, society considers that the role of the family is to:

- **avoid the end of society by ensuring the creation of new lives**
- **provide a safe and secure environment for children**
- **educate children by passing on skills and knowledge.**

In all the world religions, children are regarded as very important and all the faiths have teachings concerning parent/child relationships (**A**, **B** and **C**). Parents and children have responsibilities towards one another. Parents must accept that children have rights that should be acknowledged. Parents are clearly expected to raise their children with moral guidance.

 C Jewish teaching

Children understand their parents very well. When they see their parents consistently leading moral lives, and not out simply to satisfy their personal pleasure, they respect them and try to be like them.

Rabbi Moses Chaim Luzzato

Honour your father and your mother, so that you may live long in the land the Lord your God is giving you.

Exodus 20:12

34

Making sure that children all over the world have basic rights is the reason UNICEF (United Nations International Children's Emergency Fund) was set up in 1946. The main work of UNICEF is in developing countries where it tries to ensure that all children have access to proper health care, a balanced diet, education, clean drinking water and other basic essentials.

The rights which determine UNICEF's work were set out in the Declaration of the Rights of the Child, and accepted by the United Nations in 1959.

The basis of the Declaration is that 'mankind owes the child the best it has to give.'

The problem with 'Declarations' is that they are considered 'soft' laws because, although governments may agree to accept them, if the Declaration is broken in any way, there is very little the United Nations, or any other organisation, can do about it. This is why, in 1989, the United Nations adopted The Convention of the Rights of the Child. Countries which accept a 'Convention' are taking on a commitment which is binding and which has specific penalties for breaking any part of it.

stop and think!

The Declaration of the Rights of the Child was published in 1959 by the United Nations. The six key points were:

Children have the right to

a protection, allowing them to grow and develop

b a name and nationality

c adequate food, medical treatment and education

d love and care from parents or guardians

e protection from neglect, cruelty and danger

f protection from discrimination

In what order of importance do you think these points should be? Try to explain why you made your choices.

QUESTIONS

1 Read **A**.

  a What qualities might Jesus have seen in children that are needed by all Christians?

  b What kind of relationship do these teachings encourage between parents and children?

  c Do you agree with them?

2 How has the role of the family changed in recent years?

3 What are the main difficulties for parents and children today?

D What rights do you think this child has been deprived of?

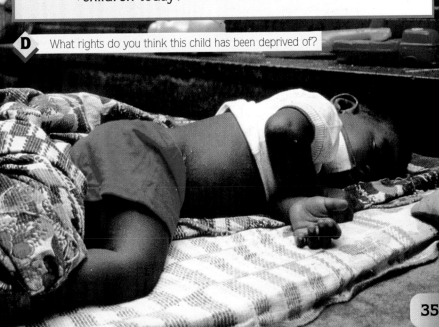

Love and

We use the word 'love' frequently when we speak, but we do not always mean the same thing by it. The experience of 'loving' our parents is clearly different from 'loving' a pet or a particular food.

The Hindus have twenty different words in Sanskrit which describe love. In the Greek language four different words are used to denote different types of love (**A**).

A Four definitions of love

Agape:

concern for the well-being and dignity of others. Different from all other types of love because it involves charity, tolerance, and respect for all people, even those we do not like. It is a purely selfless love.

Eros:

the love that is based on the physical attraction that people feel for one another. This is the state of 'falling in love'. It is based on sexual affection/passion.

Storge:

the sort of love or affection that we feel towards certain places or things.

Philos:

the kind of love that is expressed in friendships – those close to us, such as relatives and friends.

Christianity

The definition of Christian love (agape) is set out in the famous piece of writing by St Paul in his letter to the Corinthians (**B**). It demands a great deal from people, but it is the ideal which most Christians try to aspire to.

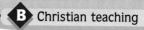
B Christian teaching

Love is patient, love is kind. It does not envy, it does not boast, it is not proud. It is not rude, it is not self-seeking, it is not easily angered, it keeps no record of wrongs. Love does not delight in evil but rejoices with the truth. It always protects, always trusts, always hopes, always perseveres.

1 Corinthians 13:4–7

However, even amongst the most secure relationships, arguments occur and difficulties can arise. All the world religions, however, recognise the need for forgiveness and would agree with the definition of love as set out in 1 Corinthians 13.

The main aspect of Jesus's teaching was the emphasis he placed on forgiveness both of friends and enemies (**C**).

C Christian teaching

You have heard that it was said, 'Love your neighbour and hate your enemy'. But I tell you: 'Love your enemies and pray for those who persecute you'.

Matthew 5:43–45

stop and think!

- How realistic is it to call on people to love their enemies?

- Are there some things which would make you finish a friendship even if you forgave the individual?

forgiveness

What is love?

Enemies of love

anger

jealousy

pride

disloyalty

flattery

intolerance

selfishness

lying

distrust

dishonesty

QUESTIONS

1 Match the photographs **C** to **F** with the four definitions of love given in **A**.

2 Give examples of four demonstrations of agape in action.

3 The 'Enemies of love' (right) can all cause disagreements: Place them in order of seriousness, and give reasons for your answers.

Love and forgiveness

Islam

In Islam, the giving of **zakah** embraces the concepts of love and forgiveness. Muslims who have a certain amount of savings are expected to pay zakat to those in need. This will be 2.5 per cent of their wealth. This 'tax' is compulsory, and is regarded as a religious duty and an act of worship. The money is used to help the poor, the disabled and the elderly. Muslims believe that giving charity is a way to make up for one's sins and to help to level the imbalances in society's wealth distribution. Some of these are described in **G**.

Zakat is one of the Five Pillars of Islam. The others are Shahadah (belief in only one God), Salah (praying five times a day), Sawm (fasting during Ramadan) and Hajj (pilgrimage to Makkah).

> **stop and think!**
> According to the Qur'an, 'Kind words and covering of faults are better than charity followed by injury.'
>
> (Qur'an surah 2: 263)
>
> • What does this tell you about the attitude Muslims are expected to have towards others?

QUESTIONS

Read through **G**.

1 List some of the qualities that Muslims believe individuals should have.

2 What suggestions are made about how these qualities can be expressed practically?

3 Suggest two ways in which a member of a caring and loving family might help another individual to make better relationships outside the family.

 G Muslim teaching

Beware of suspicion, for suspicion is a great falsehood. Do not search for faults in each other, nor yearn after that which others possess, nor envy, nor entertain malice or indifference; be servants of Allah. Visit the sick, feed the hungry and release the suffering.

Hadith

Buddhism

Buddhist teaching corresponds closely with the concept of 'agape'. True love stems not from a need or desire but rather a wish for another's wellbeing. True love avoids hurting others, it is selfless (**H**).

 H Buddhist teaching

There is no need for us to agree philosophically, no need to share a temple or a belief. If we are full of good will, our own mind, our own heart, is the temple. Kindness alone is enough. This is my religion.

Voices of Survival in the Nuclear Age, by the Dalai Lama

> **stop and think!**
> • Can you think of a person who is giving their life for others?
>
> • According to the teachings of the Buddha, there are four friends who are good hearted: the friend who will always help; the friend who is the same in happiness and disaster; the friend who gives good advice; the friend who sympathises with your problems. What sort of qualities would you expect from a good friend? Do you think that we are attracted to people like ourselves?

I Is love always unconditional?

Central to Buddhist teachings is the idea that the selfless love shown by the mother of the family closely resembles the pure love of a Buddha (**J**).

Buddhists believe that loving kindness must be extended to all the beings in the world, not just to parents and relatives.

J Buddhist teaching

My mother's kindness is responsible for all the opportunities I have... My mother always took care of me, feeding me properly, protecting me from dangers, directing my life... From the time of my conception she has been worried and concerned about me.

The Wishfulfilling Golden Sun,
by Lama Zopa Rinpoche

QUESTIONS

Look at **J**.

1 a Do Buddhists value a mother's love more than that of the father?

b Why might this be?

2 a Is a mother's love different from a father's?

b Why is it used as a model for true love?

Marriage and divorce

A

I know I've got to find,
some kind of peace of mind,
I've been looking everywhere,
Just to find someone who'll care.

Jimmy Ruffin, soul singer, What
becomes of the broken-hearted?

When Jimmy Ruffin sang these lyrics in **A** in the 1960s, he was expressing what many individuals seek in marriage. Nowadays, it often seems that marriage no longer provides 'some kind of peace of mind' for very long. With a rising divorce rate showing little sign of abating, some Christian churches and other world religions have had to reassess their stances on marriage and divorce.

B Christian teaching

[Marriage] … is a way of life that all should honour; and it must not be undertaken lightly, carelessly or selfishly, but reverently, responsibly and after serious thought.
[The couple promise to love and cherish one another] … for better, for worse, for richer, for poorer, in sickness and in health… till death us do part, according to God's holy law.
Church of England marriage ceremony

Marriage

Most religious faiths believe that sexual relationships should only take place within a permanent relationship; in other words, marriage. All the major religions view marriage as a very serious lifelong commitment (**B**).

Many of the forms of marriage service used by different Christian groups are quite distinctive, but all of them contain certain details which appear to be in common:

- a statement of what marriage is
- questions ensuring that the couple are free to marry and that they understand their responsibilities
- the taking of vows (promises)
- the exchange of rings
- the declaration that the couple are man and wife
- blessings and prayers
- the signing of the state register in front of witnesses.

C Hindu teaching

In a Hindu wedding, the couple take seven steps towards a sacred fire. Each step is believed to have special significance.

Step 1 - food

Step 2 - strength

Step 3 - increasing wealth

Step 4 - good fortune

Step 5 - children

Step 6 - the seasons

Step 7 - everlasting friendship

In Britain, the legal age requirement for marriage is 18, or 16 with parental permission. In Islamic and Hindu communities the age can be lower and many marriages are **assisted** or **arranged**. Unlike many western marriages, where the emphasis is often on love, successful marriages within these traditions are based on a shared set of values. Of course, love is seen as important, but this is something which may develop after marriage, not necessarily before. It is important to remember, as well, that arranged marriages were quite normal in Britain in past centuries. Even today, some people in western society view marriage as a 'convenience' – a way of continuing the family line, and of sharing property and money.

Being married as opposed to living together means that it is harder to just walk out on one's partner. In marriage services, whether **civil** or religious there are vows, a publicly sworn commitment to one another.

Every religious tradition approaches the marriage ceremony in a unique way but certain themes are common throughout all of them (**D**).

Normally both partners are unmarried at the time of marrying, and may only be married to one person at any one time (**monogamy**) although some religions, such as Islam, allow the man to have more than one wife (**polygamy**). Generally, however, most Muslim men marry only one.

Polygamy was more common in the past than it is today, particularly in times of war, when large numbers of men would be killed in battle. Consequently, there would be many women without husbands, and widows often faced difficulties in bringing up their children. By allowing limited polygamy, Islam ensured that these women would not struggle as one-parent families, but instead, could be offered the chance of a secure home with the full rights of a wife.

The teachings of Islam, set out clearly in the Hadith, state clearly what is important in a marriage (**E**).

D Common themes of marriage

Procreation

Permanence

P

Personal loyalty

E Muslim teaching

Do not marry only for a person's looks; their beauty might become the cause of moral decline. Do not marry for wealth, since this may become the cause for disobedience. Marry rather on the grounds of religious devotion… make it a relationship of mutual love, peace, faithfulness and co-operation.

Hadith

QUESTIONS

1 Look through the following qualities of a marriage partner and decide the order of importance.

2 Why do you think many marriages break down?

3 Describe some of the ways in which both parents and children might suffer or even benefit if a marriage breaks up.

intelligence	common interest	physical looks	generosity
patience	forgiveness	trust	sexual compatibility
faithfulness	sense of humour	practical abilities	

Marriage and divorce

Divorce

During the last few decades, divorce in every society has become increasingly common. The main world religions have had to face up to the problem and seek some kind of compromise. Some Christian churches find themselves in a dilemma over this point. Some denominations, such as Roman Catholicism, interpret particular Biblical passages about divorce in certain ways, and refuse to accept any second unions in an attempt to protect the marriage values. Others acknowledge that we live in a world where human failures can poison relationships, and accept that staying together is sometimes the worst of all possible solutions.

There are many reasons why marriages in all societies break down and why there is such an increase in the divorce rate:

- People may expect too much from marriage. When hardships occur, such as lack of money or illness, couples find it difficult to cope.

- Children (or lack of them) can cause a great amount of strain.

- Women are more likely to continue working and are often financially free from their husbands.

- Pressure from the media – extra-marital sex in films, television and magazines is presented as the 'norm'.

- Divorce is now far easier to obtain and to is no longer seen as a **stigma**.

- Individuals often get married very young and change as they grow older.

- People tend to live longer and healthier lives. In the past, second marriages often took place after a partner's death.

- Women's roles have changed – they do not necessarily want to give up work and look after children or the household.

ROYAL DIVORCE WILL GO AHEAD

No wisdom of Solomon in courts of last resort

THREE RUNAWAY SISTERS TRY TO MEND THEIR PARENTS' BROKEN MARRIAGE

The law can't save marriages

MEDIATION COULD SAVE MARRIAGES

The real problem is not how hard divorce is, but how easy it is to get married

COUPLES REFLECT ON DIVORCE

Breakdown rate

LAW AND CHURCH WELCOME END TO QUICKIE DIVORCES

How children are damaged by divorce

£50 MILLION DIVORCE

Although divorce is allowed in most religions, it is clear that it should not be taken lightly and should only be carried out after all attempts at **reconciliation** have been tried and have failed.

Islam

Islam allows a man to divorce his wife but such an action is not really approved of. Before divorcing, three things must be done:

- The couple must attempt to sort out their problems.
- If this fails, then two relatives or friends should try to mediate.
- If this does not work, then the couple must wait for four months before the marriage is ended.

Neither partner can marry for a period of time after the divorce – usually three months. This in case the woman finds that she is pregnant.

Christianity

Most Christians accept divorce, but Roman Catholics believe that a marriage cannot be broken. Instead, they allow an **annulment**. If a marriage did not take place properly then it can be cancelled (for example, if one partner was forced into the marriage, or was insane).

Different branches of the Christian Church interpret the Bible passages about divorce in different ways. All Christians agree on the importance of marriage and that all attempts at reconciliation should be made but, with the exception of the Roman Catholic Church, they all allow remarriage. However, this remarriage may not always be allowed in a church.

Hinduism

Hinduism disapproves of divorce, but it is allowed if the husband is cruel or, after fifteen years of marriage, there are no children. However, divorce is not common in Hindu society, and it can be seen as a social stigma. The more traditional Hindus still refuse to accept divorce or remarriage.

Buddhism

Buddhists accept that some marriages will fail and that, in such cases, divorce is the most sensible course of action. The divorce must go ahead as smoothly and as sensitively as possible. The Buddhist scriptures clearly state that hurting others can never bring satisfaction, but accept that divorce will involve pain for everyone concerned.

G What do you think is the message behind this poster?

stop and think!

- In your opinion, which of the following should be grounds for a divorce?

cruelty
adultery
desertion
inability to have children
insanity
physical disability
one partner sent to prison
no longer in love with the partner
unreasonable behaviour

- What do you think 'unreasonable behaviour' might include?

- What matters have to be sorted out if a couple decide to get a divorce?

43

Sexuality

A

And among His signs is this, that He created for you mates among yourselves, that you may dwell in tranquillity with them; and He has put love and mercy between your hearts.

Qur'an surah 30:21

B

When God created man, he made them in the likeness of God. He created them male and female and blessed them …

Genesis 5:1–2

The main religious traditions emphasise the special importance of sex within a permanent relationship. It is seen as the physical expression of love and commitment – something to be enjoyed. At the same time, however, people are expected to act responsibly towards themselves and society at large (A).

The roles of men and women

The physical differences between males and females are obvious (**B**).

Contrasts are frequently made between the emotional and mental conditioning of the sexes: some see females as more emotional and sensitive than their male counterparts. Others support a patriarchy, stressing that males are strong physically and should 'head' the family through wage earning.

Clearly, some of the roles of the sexes have changed and continue to evolve in most societies. It is fair to say that there is now a far greater degree of equality in men and women's sexual relationships.

In the past, religions have been criticised for upholding the patriarchy. Muslims and Christians have encountered a lot of criticism because of this.

stop and think!

- Look at C. Why might a muslim woman feel she has more freedom if she wears a chador?

- How do you react to advertisements like the one in D?

- How would you expect a person of the opposite sex to react to them?

D What is this advert trying to sell?

C Muslim woman wearing a chador

or example, critics of the Muslim faith insist that Islam does not treat men and women equally. They will use, as an example, the inheritance laws where men inherit a greater share of an estate than women. Those who support Islam point out that women benefit doubly – first by inheritance and then indirectly because the men are responsible for their upkeep. Muslims will add that western society is responsible for exploiting women – **pornography** is 'big business'. Women's bodies are draped over cars in order to attract interest and advertisements using beautiful women often create sexual stereotyping.

Christianity has also met with much criticism on the subject of male and female equality. For example, up until recently, women could not be priests. Women are still not allowed to become priests in the Roman Catholic tradition. The writings of St Paul also state that the husband is the head of the household. These, and other stances, have enraged many 'feminist' movements.

It is not helpful that many 'mixed messages' are given to young people at a time when they face many problems. Life is confusing enough without the added difficulties of puberty and the 'taboo' subject of sex (**F**).

Contraception

Followers of all the faiths tend to disagree amongst themselves over the use of **contraception**. The teachings of the world religions do not take a firm stance against large families. In fact, some see this as fulfilling God's will.

E Jewish teaching

God blessed them and said to them, 'Be fruitful and increase in number; fill the earth …'
Genesis 1:28

… he who created the heavens, he is God; he who fashioned and made the earth, he founded it; he did not create it to be empty, but formed it to be inhabited …
Isaiah 45:18

F The roles of the sexes are often confused

The majority of religions seem to be in favour of the natural forms of birth control, but remain divided on the use of artificial methods, particularly those which are seen to interfere with intercourse. However, if a woman's life were to be endangered if she became pregnant, then the use of contraception would, in most cases, be accepted.

An important distinction must be made here between birth control, contraception and family planning:

- Birth control is any method used to limit the numbers of children born to an individual or within a population.

- Contraception is the term given to all artificial and natural methods used by couples to prevent conception.

- Family planning is the term given to the deliberate limiting or spacing of births, enabling couples to choose when to have children.

45

Sexuality

One main Christian denomination, the Roman Catholic Church, refuses to accept the use of artificial contraceptives, although certain birth control methods are allowed. Here, the teachings are clear: the Roman Catholic Church urges couples to be responsible. Sexual partners should always accept that new life may result from intercourse.

In the document *Humanae Vitae* published in 1968, the leader of the Roman Catholic Church, Pope Paul VI, declared that some practices were condemned (**G**).

Most Muslim, Hindu and Buddhist teachings do not object to the use of contraception, but almost all of them insist that children should be born within marriage. Family planning clinics are established throughout the world, but certain poorer areas, with a very high **infant mortality rate**, tend to make little use of them. Some countries, such as India and China, with **population explosions**, offer incentives to have fewer children.

G Christian teaching

... which either before, or at the moment of, or after sexual intercourse is specifically intended to prevent procreation – whether as an end or a means... It is never lawful, even for the gravest reasons, to do evil that good may come of it.

Pope Paul VI

stop and think!

- What are the main reasons given for using contraception?

- Why do you think the teaching in G has divided many Roman Catholics throughout the world?

- How do certain faiths within the Christian Church regard the Biblical command 'be fruitful and increase in number'?

The Islamic faith sees contraception as a means of family planning, but it should not be continually used to prevent children. Muslims cannot find direct guidance concerning contraception in the Qur'an, but as with many **sacred** texts, it is possible to find verses to support one's position (**H**).

H Muslim teaching

... Allah intends every facility for you; He does not want to put you to difficulties.

Qur'an surah 2:185

With advances in medical technology and the widespread access to contraceptive advice, there should be fewer instances of unwanted pregnancies and yet every day we read stories of young, single mothers, some facing hopeless situations. On a global scale, the world faces an escalating population problem and, sooner or later, it will not be able to feed or support its citizens.

QUESTIONS

1 Think of advertisements you have recently seen which emphasise sex roles or portray sexuality. List them in a table like the one below:

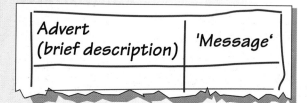

Advert (brief description)	'Message'

2 The world's population is growing at a staggering rate. Some countries actively encourage population increase, but others believe there must be a control.

a What do you think are the reasons for these different attitudes?

b Is it realistic to expect people from developing countries to limit the size of their families when it is traditional to have a large number of children?

I Methods of contraception

Artificial methods of contraception

Devices and/or chemicals to stop the sperm from reaching the ovum:

- Condom
- Diaphragm
- Cervical cap
- Spermicide
- Contraceptive sponge

Hormonal (or 'synthetic'): **progestogens** and **oestrogens**: These work by suppressing ovulation as well as acting on the cervical mucus:

- The contraceptive pill
- Implants
- Injection

Postcoital: prevents pregnancy after unprotected sex. Only used in very exceptional circumstances:

- 'Morning after' pill

Intrauterine device (IUD): inserted in the uterus to inhibit implanting of the fertilised egg.

Sterilisation/vasectomy: a reliable form of birth control but only used as a last resort as it is normally irreversible.

Natural methods of contraception

- Calendar method (prediction of a woman's **fertile** period during her menstrual cycle)
- Temperature method (the temperature of a woman's body is higher after ovulation has taken place)
- Cervical mucus (around the time of ovulation, mucus turns thin and flows more easily)
- Symptothermal (this combines the temperature and cervical mucus methods)
- Withdrawal (the male partner withdraws before ejaculation occurs – not reliable as sperm are often released before orgasm)

J Parts of the world are already very highly populated

1 What has brought about changes in the structure of the family in Britain?

2 Explain the 'roles' of husband, wife, parents and children.

3 Describe the structure of a particular type of family and the advantages and disadvantages of living within it.

4 Describe a number of advertisements in which the nuclear family is regarded as the 'normal' family.

5 Sometimes people behave quite differently at home from the way they behave with others. Give examples of this and say why you think this happens.

6 What do Islam and Christianity teach about the family?

7 Explain the main problems that face a Christian family in today's society. How do Christians respond to these problems?

8 'If men and women are to live the same lives, the family must be abolished.' Plato 300 BC. How far do you agree with this statement?

9 'All happy families resemble one another, but each unhappy family is unhappy in its own way.' Leo Tolstoy 1828–1910. What do you think Tolstoy means by his comment?

10 Which four words did the Greeks use for love? What did they mean by them?

11 Read 1 Corinthians 13 and make a list of the ten qualities of love described in the passage.

12 What modern examples can you give of people who come close to carrying out the Christian ideals of love and forgiveness?

13 What did Jesus teach about the way in which Christians should treat their enemies?

14 Would you consider it weakness to forgive? Can you forgive and still punish?

15 Describe occasions when, acting out of love, you might be offending others or even breaking the law.

16 What is the difference between liking and loving? How might a Christian love someone who has done them harm?

17 What qualities would you expect to find in a friend? Do you think it is difficult to be friends with someone who has more money than you, or is of a different religion or has different coloured skin?

18 'Even my close friend, whom I trusted, he who shared my bread, has lifted up his heel against me.' (Psalm 41:9) Why do friendships sometimes break up? Why is this a particularly painful experience?

19 Discuss how the Buddhist view of love differs from other views.

20 'All the people in the world are equal and should be treated the same.' Do you agree? Give reasons to support your answer and show that you have thought about different points of view.

 21 What do the following terms mean:
a monogamy
b polygamy

 22 State three reasons why the religious traditions support marriage.

 23 Give a brief account of the main elements of a Christian marriage ceremony.

 24 Compare the marriage ceremony of two different religions. List common elements and differences.

 25 In some traditions, marriages are 'arranged'. Do you think this is a good idea?

 26 Within a Muslim marriage, the husband and wife have separate, but equally important, roles.

'The best of treasures is a good wife. She is pleasing to her husband's eyes, obedient to his word and watchful over his possessions in his absence; and the best of you are those who treat their wives best.' *Hadith*

Use this quotation to describe the desired qualities of:
a a Muslim wife
b a Muslim husband

 27 Why do Muslims have to wait for three months after their divorce before marrying again?

 28 'The real problem isn't how hard divorce is, but how easy it is to get married.' Do you agree with this statement? Give reasons for your answer.

 29 From the religious viewpoints you have studied, explain what should happen when marriages break down.

 30 What is meant by the terms 'birth control', 'family planning' and 'contraception'?

 31 Do you think that men and women are equal in the following areas? Give reasons to support your views.
a the workplace
b relationships
c the home

 32 Do you think that things have changed much in recent years regarding who does what at home?

 33 What do you think are the main reasons why some household jobs are done primarily by men and others by women?

 34 Do you think the Roman Catholic Church is too severe in its teachings on contraception? Give reasons for your answer.

 35 How is it possible for Christians to hold such different views on birth control?

36 Should contraceptives be easily available to young people without their parents' knowledge?

Introduction
One world

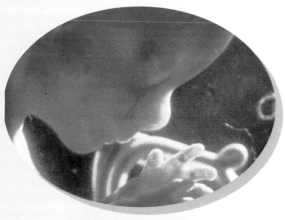

NHS Organ Donor Register

donorcard

I want to help others to live in the event of my death Please let your relatives know your wishes

Unit aims

The main aim this unit is to introduce you to the 'medical **ethics** debate' through an examination of some of the key issues stemming from medical advances. You should be aware of legal facts and moral factors concerning these issues, and recognise the influence of religious teachings and ideas, including differences of viewpoint within the same religious tradition.

Key concepts

Many religions have difficulty in adapting and coping with change. The developments in medical technology over the past twenty years have forced the world faiths to re-examine their teachings about life and death, in particular the traditional sanctity of life principle. Religious leaders, in the face of rapid advances in medical ethics, are now trying to offer guidelines to their followers, while at the same time making sure that there are safeguards against abuse.

What is this unit about?

Religious believers can find themselves in a very difficult position when confronted with issues raised by advances in medicine. One controversial area in medical ethics, which frequently arises in debate, is the subject of abortion. Medical technology can now predict potential problems in pregnancy with far greater accuracy than ever before but the issue remains largely the same as in years past.

In the last twenty-five years alone, medicine has created techniques which allow us to live without our own lungs, kidneys or heart. Even the brain can be 'replaced' by machinery which allows all our organs to function. The definition of the 'natural dying process' has had to be revised. Now individuals in a persistent vegetative state (PVS) can easily be kept 'alive'.

many choices

We will see how 'halfway technologies' – those that do not cure, but merely delay death – are on a steady increase and have brought about a total reshaping of certain medical issues. The anti-euthanasia lobby of many religious traditions, will argue that 'God gives life and only God can take it away.' Those who argue for euthanasia will point out that perhaps the problem is made more difficult because 'doctors play God' and we can become confused over where precisely life ends.

When we are healthy, we can face extreme suffering and anxiety with the knowledge that we can endure the pain, sort out the situation and then carry on with life as normal. The picture is completely changed when the illness is terminal, as can be the case with cancer. The creation of the hospice movement has gone some way to help individuals facing such futures.

In recent years, developments in embryology and genetics have prompted many uncomfortable questions not just for religious people but also for medical authorities, the courts and governments. Science is clearly going into uncharted moral territory and there is no one body helping us to decide how to act. Decisions in such matters should never be taken lightly nor can they be taken in isolation. Hospitals are limited in funding, resources and operations are costly. It is easy to affirm the right to life but how far do we go to defend and promote this right?

Medical

A   Is a foetus a human being?

There is always a lot of discussion about medical ethics as people's beliefs about life and death are different. People have different opinions, too, about what quality of life to expect and the rights of the individual to determine this. Religious groups play a large part in influencing people's opinions in these matters.

What is the nature of life?

According to the Oxford dictionary, life is 'the state of ceaseless change and functional activity peculiar to organised matter'.

The exact moment that life begins is very important when dealing with issues like abortion or experimentation on embryos. Some people refer to 'the primitive streak', the period from conception to the fifteenth day when it is possible for a fertilised ovum to split several times or even rejoin. Most religions consider that God determines the moment of conception. The medical terms for the different stages of development are:

Pre-embryo	Embryo	Foetus
conception to 2 weeks	2 weeks to 8 weeks	8 weeks onwards

The advances in medical technology witnessed over the last two decades have re-focused the debate on the 'mystery of life'. We can now see potential medical problems in foetuses; we can keep people alive on life support machines who would otherwise die; 'designer' animals and even humans are now within our grasp; hundreds of new treatments are now possible. The mystery of life appears to be increasingly explained as every month brings fresh discoveries. In the face of such advances, the major world faiths accept that there are profound religious and spiritual questions to face, one of which is: When does life begin and when does it end?

stop and think!

- When do you think life begins?
- What do you base your opinion on?
- Is it possible to hold more than one opinion on the nature of life?

ethics

When is the moment of death?

In order to sustain independent life, without any artificial means of support, the heart, the lungs and the brain must be fully functional.

This raises questions about life support systems, and will influence the decision to withdraw that support if it appears that one major organ in a patient will never fully function without it.

One really important question to consider is: Who should make the decisions in life and death situations?

- The medical profession?
- Scientists?
- Legal experts?
- The government of a country?
- Representatives of religious groups?
- The patient?
- The patient's family?
- Some combination of all these?

Another question to consider is: When should a person be declared dead, and who decides?

 Hindu teaching

Hindus feel profoundly the sanctity of every life, and bringing one into [being] is for them a sacred act. Even before the parents unite, they pray to be entrusted with the type of child they believe they could best love and help. Thus the first step is taken when the life has not yet entered the womb. For the second and third steps, during the mother's pregnancy, selected foods are given to her, and meditation is practised to create the right atmosphere for the coming child.

Yorke Crompton, Hinduism,
Ward Lock Educational, 1980

C Christian teaching

In the Church's tradition, that the principle of respect for human life from conception has been constant since its early days is well documented by recent historical studies.

Dr Teresa Iglesias, Essays in Medical Ethics,
from Christian Theology Trust

D Jewish teaching

You created my inmost being; you knit me together in my mother's womb... My frame was not hidden from you when I was made in the secret place. When I was woven together in the depths of the earth, your eyes saw my unformed body ...

Psalm 139:13,15,16

stop and think!

- **What do you think are the most important factors to consider when deciding whether to switch off a person's life support machine?**

- **Is all life sacred?**

QUESTIONS

1 Reference is often made to 'clinical' death. What is the difference between 'clinical' death and 'real' or 'actual' death?

2 Should doctors always maintain life if there is the technology available?

3 People with pacemakers can lead a virtually normal life, but without them they would die. Where should dependence on technology end?

Abortion

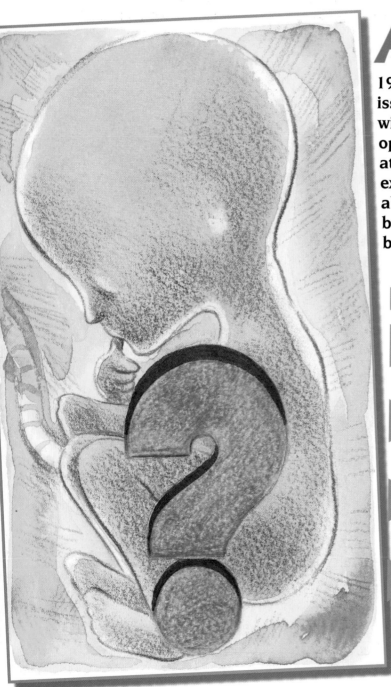

Abortion, the 'premature expulsion of the foetus from the womb', is not a new issue, but it has only been legal in Britain since 1967. Abortion is a very high profile moral issue and something which cannot be debated without feelings being involved. A person's opinions are determined by their beliefs, attitudes, experience and circumstances. For example there are those who would argue that abortion is permissible in the case of rape, but debatable when the woman has chosen to be in a sexual relationship.

When does life begin?

> Life begins at the exact moment when the sperm fuses with the egg (ovum).

> Life begins at the moment when the fertilised egg is safely lodged in the womb.

> Life begins at the moment when the baby, if born prematurely, could sustain life outside the womb.

> Life begins at the moment of birth.

A Human development

6 weeks
Human embryo. Limbs start to form. All internal organs, such as liver and stomach, have begun to form. The heart has been beating for 3 weeks.

9 weeks
The embryo has now become a foetus. The liver, kidneys, stomach and brain all function, and brainwaves can be detected. Fingers, toes and teeth buds are beginning to form. It is starting to move.

12 weeks
Eyelids and ears are fully developed. The foetus can suck its thumb and fingers.

18 weeks
Fingernails and eyelashes have formed. The foetus is very active.

16 weeks
The head has human features. Sexual organs and vocal chords have formed.

14 weeks
The foetus is breathing in and out the fluid which gives it its nutrients.

24 weeks
25 per cent or more babies survive outside the womb, provided they are given sufficient medical care.

Abortion: whose choice?

Many people think that the choice should be made by the pregnant woman, but is she the only one with rights in this case? Some people feel that the father should have a voice in the matter. They argue that society has been so concerned to ensure the rights of women, that men no longer have any rights.

stop and think!

- Abortion laws in the European Union vary from country to country. Why do you think this is?

Abortion

The legal position

In 1967 the Abortion Act was launched in the UK to prevent the increasing numbers of so-called 'back-street' or illegal abortions.

The Abortion Act (1967)

An abortion may be performed legally if two or more doctors certify that:

1 The mental or physical health of the woman or her existing children will suffer if the pregnancy continues, or

2 The child, if born, would be seriously physically or mentally handicapped.

No time limit was set but under normal circumstances the pregnancy should not have passed the 28th week.

As well as for the situations covered in the Abortion Act, there are many other reasons why a woman may seek an abortion, although in some cases the foetus may be perfectly healthy. Some reasons might be:

● to continue with the pregnancy would destroy or totally change the woman's plans for the future

● the woman would be unable to support the child financially and/or care for the child emotionally – she may be very young

● the woman may be afraid of rejecting the child, particularly in the case of rape.

There are also varying opinions on the rights of the mother versus the rights of the child. A number of organisations offer advice and support for different situations. Some will help with abortions, others are actively against it.

stop and think!

● Why *do* you think the 1967 Abortion Act was seen as necessary?

● Why *do* you think it was changed in 1990?

The Human Fertilisation and Embryology Act (1990)

As for the 1967 Act except that the time limit was reduced to 24 weeks.

QUESTIONS

Look through the information above on the Abortion Act, then read the statements below. Try and determine whether an abortion would be allowed under the 1990 law for the following:

a An amniocentisis test showing that the baby has a serious deformity.

b The baby is a result of rape.

c The parents are extremely poor and cannot afford a child.

d Through scanning, the sex of the baby has been established as female and the parents want a boy.

e The mother's life would be put at risk if the pregnancy went to full term.

f The parents are both in their late forties.

A pro-life organisation: Life

Life is a voluntary organisation made up of people of all beliefs and political persuasions. They are opposed to abortion because they believe that all life begins at conception (fertilisation), and that all life should be protected from that moment until death from natural causes. They maintain that the deliberate killing of unborn human life is always wrong, and that the foetus, whether wanted or not, should have the full protection of the law.

> It's my body and my decision. No one else should decide for me.

A pro-choice organisation: BPAS

The British Pregnancy Advisory Service is a non profit making charitable organisation founded in 1967. Since then, BPAS has helped over 400,000 women faced with unplanned pregnancy. As an organisation BPAS believes that the right choice is the woman's personal choice. It does not campaign for or against abortion but believes that it is essential that abortion remains legal because women who feel unable to continue with a pregnancy will often risk their health or life to end it. The alternatives to legal abortion are 'back street' or self-induced attempts for those unable to afford expensive visits abroad.

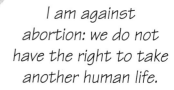

> I am against abortion: we do not have the right to take another human life.

> Instead of wasting time, energy and money campaigning for or against abortion, we should be trying to ensure that all children who are born have a decent life.

B Some of the many views on abortion

QUESTIONS

1 Make a list of the three main arguments for and against abortion.

2 Should the father have any rights in the matter of abortion, or is it solely the woman's decision?

57

Abortion

C Jewish teaching

So God created man in His own image.
Genesis 1:27

You shall not murder.
Exodus 20:13

The word of the Lord came to me, saying, 'Before I formed you in the womb I knew you, before you were born I set you apart...'
Jeremiah 1:4–5

Judaism

Jews believe that all life comes from God, and that human beings are born in his image. Human beings, as the pinnacle of God's creation, have been given the responsibility to care for all life. Jews have tried to explain the special relationship between God and human beings by suggesting that human life has been sanctified (**C**).

D Christian teaching

The Roman Catholic Church tends not only to reaffirm the right to life – the violation of which is an offence against the human person and against God the Creator and Father, the loving source of all life – but she also intends to devote herself ever more fully to concrete defence and promotion of this right.

Letter on combatting abortion and euthanasia, Pope John Paul II, 19 May 1991

We have been created by Almighty God in His image and likeness. No pregnancy is unplanned, because no baby can be conceived unless Almighty God intends that conception and has willed that particular and completely unique person into existence. The merciless slaughter of unborn babies is never justified.

Based on Catechism of the Catholic Church, Catholic Truth Society, 1990

Christianity

There is no one Christian view on abortion and individual Christians may not even totally agree with their denomination's official stance.

The Roman Catholic and Orthodox Churches forbid abortion (**D**). The official Canon Law of the Roman Catholic Church states that anyone who commits the sin of abortion automatically **excommunicates** themselves from the Church. However, the Roman Catholic Church does preach an attitude of love and support, not condemnation, for those who have had an abortion.

The Church of England and most Protestant Churches agree with the Roman Catholic and Orthodox stance in principle, but are prepared to allow abortion in certain circumstances and leave more to the conscience of the individual (**E**). Such circumstances would be in the case of rape, serious risk to the mother's life, or serious risk of disability.

E Christian teaching

We affirm that every human life, created in the divine image, is unique... and that holds for each of us, born or yet to be born... Although the foetus is to be specially respected and protected, nonetheless the life of the foetus is not absolutely paramount.
Church of England Report, 1984

Circumstances which may often justify an abortion are direct threats to the life of the mother, or the probable birth of a severely abnormal child. The woman's other children, bad housing and family poverty should also be considered.
Methodist Synod, 1976

Islam

The official Muslim view on abortion is clear: since life is a gift from Allah, abortion is a sin (**F**). However, some Muslim doctors believe that abortion can be legal when the foetus in the womb threatens the mother's life. In the Muslim faith, the mother's life takes precedence over the baby's, and the reasons for this are clear – the mother has many responsibilities and duties, and, although regrettable, an abortion will be less disruptive to the family than the mother's death.

Generally, life is seen as a gift from God and should only be regarded as a loan to humanity and not as a possession. As life is only on loan, it is not ours to do with as we like, but must be cared for and protected.

Hinduism

Hindus believe that all life is sacred, so there should be no interference with the natural processes. All life forms have their source in God, and, although Hinduism does not have a central authority, abortion would not normally be acceptable (**G**). However, it might be considered if the mother's life is at risk.

stop and think!

Jesus asked his followers to love one another. In what circumstances might a Christian feel that allowing an abortion might be an act of love?

F Muslim teaching

Do not kill your children in fear of poverty. We shall provide for both them and you. Killing them is a big sin.

Qur'an surah 6:151

G Hindu teaching

His being is the source of all being, the seed of all things that in this life have their life... He is God, hidden in all beings... He watches the works of Creation, lives in all things, watches all things.

Svetasvatara Upanishad

In Him all things exist, from Him all things originate. He has become all.

Mahabharata Shanti Parva 47-56

QUESTIONS

1. Is abortion the deliberate taking of life?

2. Might there be occasions when abortion is acceptable?

3. What are the effects of abortion on society?

4. What is the key idea underlying religious objections to abortion?

5. **a** Why do you think that there is no agreed view of abortion among Christians?

   b Would it be a help or a hindrance to have just one agreed view?

6. Has your opinion changed on abortion changed since studying this unit? If so, in what ways?

Adoption

Although abortion may be a sensible decision for a woman to take when faced with an unwanted baby, some other people strongly disagree, saying that there is always the alternative of adoption. There are thousands of couples in Britain who cannot have a baby of their own and who are desperate to adopt. However, the increasing number of abortions has made adoption much more difficult.

In favour of adoption

- The child will be given the chance of life.
- The mother will not have to live with the physical and mental after effects of abortion.
- The child will be received into a loving home knowing that he or she is wanted.

Against adoption

- The mother may find it hard to give the child away. There might be many guilty feelings.
- The child might not have a true sense of identity. He or she may feel rejected.
- The mother might always wonder and worry about her child.
- The mother might change her mind and want the child back.

Quite clearly, there is a constant theme running through all the teachings of the world faiths regarding care for children and the needy. If children have lost their parents, other families are expected to show compassion and to rally around and take care of them. At the same time, these children must never be misled about their background and parentage.

Judaism

In Judaism, the positive attitude towards adoption is seen in the story of Esther. She was adopted at a young age, and became a heroine in Jewish history when she saved her people from being killed (**A**).

Islam

Although Muslims are encouraged to foster children who have been orphaned or abandoned, certain difficulties arise over official adoption because such procedures, in the eyes of civil law, would give the adopted child the same status as a natural child born to the couple.

This legal recognition would create problems in the light of some Islamic beliefs. When an adopted son reached puberty, for example, he would not be able to mix socially with the women of his household, because he was not related to them by blood. The women would have to wear full Islamic dress in front of him, but not in front of their own sons or nephews (**B**).

Hinduism

For Hindus, in particular, the question of adoption is slightly more problematic because of the caste system. Although the system was officially abolished in 1950, it still governs many aspects of Hindu life. Hindus have no worries about adopting from relatives because this takes away any doubts about the child's ancestry and inheritance. The religious teachings remind Hindus of their duty to respect all people, regardless of their background (**C**).

The organisation Life clearly believes the decision to give a child up for adoption is not an easy one, but it is an unselfish and caring decision to give the unborn child the chance of life. As such, it is a responsible and caring choice. In its research on adoption procedures, Life has praised the number of adoption agencies that take tremendous care over the vetting of prospective parents and the matching of children to families.

A Jewish teaching

This girl... known as Esther, was lovely in form and features, and Mordecai had taken her as his own daughter when her father and mother died.

Esther 2:7

B Muslim teaching

Nor has He made your adopted sons your sons... Call them by (the names of) their fathers: that is juster in the sight of Allah.

Qur'an surah 33:4

C Hindu teaching

Children are loved not for their own sake, but because the Self lives in them... Everything is loved not for its own sake, but because the Self lives in it ...

Brihadaranyaka Upanishad 4:6

stop and think!

As an adopted child gets older, what difficulties do you think could arise for:
- the adopted child?
- the adoptive parents?
- the natural parents?

QUESTIONS

1 Do you agree with Life that adoption is a 'responsible and caring choice'?

2 Read **D**.

  a Is it possible to guarantee that all adopted children will be happy?

  b Is it realistic to think that all adoptive parents would be this open? Is such openness necessarily a good thing?

D An adopted child's view

My adoptive parents were really open with me and I grew up knowing that I had natural parents, but that the people I called Mum and Dad had chosen me specially.

Hi-tech babies

ONE WORLD 3 MANY CHOICES Hi-tech babies

stop and think!

The fertility methods described on this page are considered to be perfectly acceptable by many people. What are your thoughts about them?

BRAVE NEW BABIES

Born or made?

New agony over surrogate twins

Vatican in test-tube baby row

stop and think!

- How do these medical 'advances' fit in with the concept of God as the sole creator and sustainer of life?

There are many medical techniques for assisting conceptions, some of which continue to cause a lot of controversy.

Assisted conception techniques

Test-tube babies
Officially called in vitro fertilisation or IVF, it was developed to enable women with blocked fallopian tubes to have children. The woman is given drugs to help her produce eggs which are collected and fertilised by sperm. As long as fertilisation has taken place, about three eggs are usually placed back in the womb.

Embryo freezing
A large number of women have had eggs or embryos frozen in case they are needed in the future. There is a legal time limit on how long these eggs and embryos can be kept. One problem is that when the time limit is reached, many women cannot be contacted to be advised that their eggs or embryos must now be used or destroyed.

AID (artificial insemination by donor)
This has been practised in Britain for about 50 years. Donor sperm is introduced into the neck of the womb. It takes, on average, three attempts before pregnancy occurs. Compared with other fertility treatments, it is the simplest and cheapest. As British law stands at present, the identity of the donor is kept secret, and the child's birth certificate has the husband or partner's name as the father.

Fertility drugs
Over the last few decades there have been amazing developments in fertility drugs. Many women with fertility problems are given drugs which help to encourage ovulation. One of the worrying side effects is the increased risk of multiple births.

Genetic engineering

Although scientists are learning more and more about the 'make-up' of genes, they are, at present, unable to change them. Research into **genetic engineering** is concentrating on identifying the genes that cause hereditary diseases such as **Down's Syndrome**, with the idea that these genes could be replaced with ones from another healthy human, or from animals.

One example using animals, which appears to have met with success, is the research into emphysema – at present, an incurable condition in which human lungs deteriorate. The disease is caused by smoking, airborne pollution or sometimes through inherited **DNA**. Large amounts of **AAT** can protect lung tissue from attack but this can only be derived from large quantities of human blood. In 1990, researchers from Edinburgh managed to transplant the gene that makes AAT into 'Tracy', a sheep. Tracy now produces milk that contains AAT which can be used in treating emphysema. Tracy is extremely well looked after, and lives a pampered life. This is a good example of the use of genetic engineering, where scientists are sure that the potential risks have been minimised or eliminated.

Eugenics (sex preselection)

At present, you can only try to determine the sex of a child by creating an acidic or alkaline environment in the womb, and this is not a guaranteed method. If genetic research on animals ever leads to the ability to alter the genes which determine the sex of offspring, it might, in the future, be possible for farmers to produce more cows than bulls, and for parents to choose to have a boy rather than a girl or vice versa.

stop and think!

Can you think of any advantages and disadvantages in being able to choose the sex of a child?

Cloning

Cloning occurs naturally in the case of identical twins. Artificial cloning would mean exchanging the nucleus in a fertilised egg with a nucleus from a donor's body cell. The egg is then implanted into the womb of a surrogate mother and allowed to go through a natural birth. The resulting child would be genetically identical to the donor. At present, the cloning of human beings is still a long way away (in Britain, cloning of humans is illegal). It is important to stress that the 'child' clone is *not* the same person as the 'parent' clone. To suggest that if we are cloned, we can live forever, implies that we are no more than our DNA and we thereby deny an essential part of our humanity. We are the sum of our experiences and life histories: we are much more than our genes.

Another sheep regarded as important by the medical world is Dolly! Dolly brought the issue of cloning very much to the media's attention in 1996.

A 'Dolly', the first animal to be cloned in Britain

Ectogenesis (glass womb)

Research has produced artificial wombs capable of sustaining the life of a foetus for a few days. At the other end of the development of a child, the advances in incubator technology mean that babies born as much as three months early are now surviving.

Many people are concerned that the teachings of the world faiths are ill prepared to deal with these breathtaking developments in genetics and biotechnology. Some representatives of the world religions accept the fact that their holy scriptures do not give much guidance on such matters (**B**).

 B Sikh teaching

I don't think there are any passages in the Adi Granth touching these subjects, particularly because they were not well known or an order of the day… The Sikhs these days would normally follow the general trend of society and are liberal and broadminded, excepting the very orthodox element.

Dr Chatwal, Secretary of the Sikh Cultural Society

Some scientists, with total equanimity, talk of a future where children could be products of three different sets of parents: biological, gestational and nurturers. If these three relationships are separated, we will undermine the essence of something which is specifically human (**C**).

 C Christian teaching

There are undoubted benefits which gene therapy might bring. I do fear for the future, however, if the language of bodily human love is gradually replaced by an artificial process, if procreation becomes production, or even reproduction, and if the individual human being becomes valued as a product to be ordered rather than a gift to be received.

Cardinal Basil Hume, Creation and Procreation: We tread on holy ground, The Independent 15.3.97

Hindus would say that medical technology only fits with respect for life (Ahimsa) if the motive is totally selfless, and brings about some spiritual benefit.

D Hindu teaching

The result of a virtuous action is pure joy; actions done out of passion bring pain and suffering; ignorance arises from actions motivated by 'dark' intentions.

Bhagavad Gita 14:16

The Warnock Report

The Report, published in July 1984, made several far-reaching recommendations, some of which are given below:

- All research and treatment of infertility should be licensed by an independent body.

- No experiments should be carried out on embryos more than 14 days old and no embryo used for research should be implanted into a human womb.

- No human embryo should be implanted in the womb of another animal.

- It should be a criminal offence to set up surrogacy agencies on a commercial basis.

Religious leaders are in no doubt that there are specific barriers which we cannot cross without altering the way in which we relate to others. They also warn against the potential dangers which could follow from such 'advances'.

Britain and the Warnock Report

In 1982, the government set up a special enquiry into In Vitro Fertilisation and Embryo Experimentation. The committee of fifteen experts included doctors, lawyers, scientists, psychologists and childcare specialists. They were asked to consider:

- recent and potential developments
- their social, ethical and legal implications, and
- what policies and safeguards should be applied for their use.

Chairing the committee was Dame Mary Warnock, a philosopher.

This report is very significant because it deals with matters of life and death, and the effect that such things have on the whole of society. The Warnock Committee looked at the subject of test-tube babies, at artificial insemination, and at egg donation. They also considered the freezing of test-tube embryos for future use, genetic engineering and cloning, clinical intervention in the genes and **chromosomes** of embryos and womb leasing. One of the most difficult issues considered was **surrogacy**.

The other major area covered by this report was the creation of embryos for medical research. Doctors insist that experimental research on these embryos provides a vital means of advancing medical knowledge and treatment. The Warnock Committee had to decide at what point in an embryo's life such experiments should cease.

Views on this vary greatly. Roman Catholics believe that an embryo's life is sacred from the moment of conception and therefore disagree with all experimentation, whilst medical bodies like the Royal Colleges and the Medical Research Council draw the line at different points in the first days or weeks after conception.

stop and think!

- So, what was the Committee to do? Whose voice were they to listen to? What do you think?

In recommending new legislation or regulations, the Committee sought to embody the 'minimum moral requirement' of this society.

Religious viewpoints

There are several principles which are shared by most of the major religions (**E**, **F** and **G**):

- all life is sacred
- each individual has intrinsic value and dignity
- marriage is sacred
- each natural species is distinct.

Moral viewpoints

There are also several key moral beliefs amongst religions that affect any aspect of reproductive engineering:

- any infertility treatment involving a third party can lead to a form of adultery, and certainly will involve a breach of marriage. Where family members are involved it could, technically, be considered to be **incest.**
- in addition, there will be problems in 'legitimising' any child born in such a way.
- embryos should not be produced specifically for research because this devalues life.
- mankind should not attempt to 'play God' in creating life contrary to nature, but should work to ensure that our increasing power over nature is used responsibly and with due reverence for life.
- experimentation with animal/human mixtures is either specifically (as in the Old Testament book of Leviticus) or generally condemned.

 Buddhist teaching

Each being is related to us ourselves, just as our own parents are related to us in this life. We regard our survival as an inalienable right. As co-inhabitants of this planet, other species too have this right to survival.

The Buddhist Declaration on Nature

 Hindu teaching

I look upon all creatures equally; none are less dear to me and none more dear.

Bhagavad Gita 9:29

G **Christian teaching**

Right from the beginning, we are conceived and nurtured in a setting of human relatedness; if that is denied us, then a crucial aspect of personhood is denied and we are less than properly human… marriage should be understood as primarily a unique human relationship intended by God to be permanent.

Richard Jones, Groundwork of Christian Ethics, *Epworth Press, 1991*

H

A surrogate mother relates her pride at having a friend's babies

Holding her baby daughter, the real mother shared her delight with the surrogate mother who made the birth possible.

After twelve childless years of marriage, Tracey and Colin Wells were overjoyed when Fiona Burton, acting as a host mother, gave birth to twin boys in April 1994. When asked why she did it, Fiona replied, 'It was one of the best experiences of my life. I was walking on air for weeks after I'd given birth to the twins. I did it for my friend. Just to see the happiness on her face made it all worthwhile.'

Unfortunately, one of the twins died of meningitis shortly after his birth but just over a year later, Fiona agreed to bear a second child for her best friend, and in August 1995 she gave birth to a little girl. When interviewed she said, 'I have absolutely no regrets as I was only the carrier. They were hi-tech babies born as a result of embryos produced by the eggs and sperm of Tracey and Colin that were implanted in me.'

By Angella Johnson, 'I did it for my friend' (The Guardian, *11 April 1996*)

QUESTIONS

1 Read **H**.

a How easy do you think it really would be to hand the babies over?

b We are told that the babies were conceived as a result of embryos implanted in the surrogate mother.

Do you think this might have made a difference to the way Fiona felt about the babies?

c 'No one can match giving the gift of life.' Do you agree?

d Explain what might be some of the dangers and problems of surrogacy.

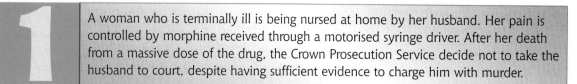

Euthanasia

What is euthanasia? The word literally implies a gentle and easy death, but is the premature ending of life necessarily the right thing to do? Those involved in caring for the terminally ill would probably not agree. Nonetheless, there are those who campaign for 'assisted suicide' to be made legal.

Consider the following case studies. If you were involved in any of these cases, what questions would you be asking?

Case Studies

1 A woman who is terminally ill is being nursed at home by her husband. Her pain is controlled by morphine received through a motorised syringe driver. After her death from a massive dose of the drug, the Crown Prosecution Service decide not to take the husband to court, despite having sufficient evidence to charge him with murder.

2 After an elderly patient dies, nursing staff begin to realise that her heroin syringes have been running out much faster after her daughter, a qualified nurse, has been to visit. However, the coroner records that the patient died from bronchial pneumonia which was as a result of the illness, not of the drug. Despite confessing to the medical staff what she had done, it was decided that there was no case to answer.

3 A doctor treating an elderly, bed-ridden patient at home, leaves powerful sleeping tablets by the bed with strict instructions that no more than two must be taken on any account. The patient has already told the doctor that she wants to die.

4 A consultant rheumatologist from Winchester made huge headlines when he was convicted of attempted murder, but given a 12-month suspended sentence in 1992. His 'crime' had been to give a terminally ill, elderly woman a lethal injection of potassium chloride. She had requested this, and her decision had been fully supported by her two sons.

5 A badly deformed baby is born and needs immediate maximum intensive care to survive. The mother also needs urgent medical care, and the doctor deliberately deals with her needs first.

stop and think!

- How do these case studies differ from the situation where the decision is made to turn off a life support system?
- It has been said that euthanasia is an 'open secret' in Britain. What do think is meant by this statement, and do you agree with it?

Christianity

Christians do not hold one particular view on whether people should be allowed to take their own lives. However, there are principles on which most would agree:

- Human life is a gift from God – as such it is sacred, has dignity and is his possession.
- Death is an event in eternal life, not an end in itself – whilst the physical body dies, the soul lives on.
- People should receive good terminal care – all the patient's needs, including the spiritual, should be met.

Islam

Muslims totally reject the idea of euthanasia on the following grounds:

- Every soul is perfect even if the body is not.
- The reason for all suffering is known to Allah.
- All suffering has a purpose – Allah is not unfair.
- Allah has decided each person's life span and so the length of life is not a personal choice.
- 'Mercy killing' may not be the person's choice.

 A Sikh teaching

The dawn of a new day is the herald of a sunset. Earth is not thy permanent home. Life is like a shadow on a wall. All thy friends have departed. Thou too must go.

The Suhi of Ravidas

Sikhism

It has been suggested that the problem of voluntary euthanasia is not so acute in less developed countries which do not have as many hospitals or the sophisticated medical technology to keep people alive for an indeterminate length of time. Sikhism, for example, believes that the quality of life, not its length, is what should concern us. For Sikhs, death is not to be feared, it is not the end of life (**A**).

QUESTIONS

1 Every year there are cases of relatives, friends or doctors who are found guilty of assisting someone else to die. Should Case study 1 be any different, and how should such a decision be made?

2 Was the daughter in Case study 2 right to act in this way? Do you think this case would have been handled any differently if the daughter had not been a nurse or if the patient had been younger?

3 Was the doctor in Case study 3 right to leave the tablets, knowing how the patient felt? Is this the same as administering a larger than normal dose of painkillers by syringe at the patient's request?

4 In Case study 5:
  a Is the delay in treating the baby the same as 'causing its death'?
  b Would it have been different if the mother hadn't needed such skilled medical treatment?

5 Although euthanasia is illegal, very few prosecutions have taken place. When they have, the punishment has most usually been probation or a suspended sentence. Is there any point to this?

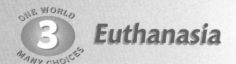

Euthanasia

The legal position

In Britain there are no laws dealing directly with euthanasia. Currently it is covered by the laws forbidding **murder.** Murder is, of course, punishable by life imprisonment, but test cases regarding euthanasia have often reduced the charge to attempted murder or **manslaughter**.

Homicide Act (1957)

This applies in England and Wales. Scotland has a similar law.

Three sections of the Act are particularly relevant:

Section 2(1) If a person is considered to be suffering from some abnormality of the mind that would affect his mental responsibility, he shall not be convicted of murder even if he has killed or was party to the killing of another person.

Section 2(3) This is usually referred to as **diminished responsibility** and instead the charge will be manslaughter.

Section 4(1) It will also be manslaughter, not murder, if the person is involved in a suicide pact with another person or persons.

In 1976, the Criminal Laws Revision Committee suggested that there should be a new offence (to replace murder) for those who, from compassion, kill another person if that person is:
- permanently subject to great bodily pain or suffering, or
- permanently helpless from bodily or mental incapacity, or
- subject to rapid and incurable bodily or mental degeneration.

The proposal would not necessarily have required the previous consent of the deceased and would carry a maximum penalty of two years imprisonment but, despite considerable support, the suggestion was dropped.

Suicide Act (1961)

Suicide has not been a crime in England and Wales since 1961, but assisting it is still criminal.

Two relevant sections apply:

Section 2(1) A person who encourages, assists, or gets someone else to assist another in attempting suicide will, if convicted, face a maximum sentence of 14 years imprisonment.

Section 2(2) If a person being tried for murder or manslaughter is proved to have encouraged, assisted, or got someone else to assist, suicide, then the jury can find them guilty of this second offence.

The position in other countries

The Netherlands

In 1984, the Netherlands Medical Association accepted guidelines for the practice of voluntary euthanasia. In 1990, the Solicitor General announced a procedure for reporting voluntary euthanasia to the coroner. Provided that the guidelines have been strictly followed, the doctors are not liable to prosecution. This procedure was legalised in 1993.

stop
and
think!

- Despite the fact that suicide is no longer an offence, 'assisted' suicide still is. What is your opinion of this?

stop
and
think!

- Many people feel that Britain should follow the Netherlands' lead in voluntary euthanasia. What do you think?

Australia

In September 1996, history was made when an elderly prostate cancer patient became the world's first legally assisted suicide. Bob Dent took his life at his home in Darwin, Australia, taking advantage of the unique Northern Territory's Rights of the Terminally Ill Act which had been passed as law some time before. After consultation with his wife, and having persuaded his three doctors that his case was hopeless, he chose a time and asked for assistance in using the 'Deliverance Program', alternatively known as the 'Death Machine'. Mr Dent was allowed to use a computer to self-administer a lethal injection of barbiturates and a muscle relaxant into his bloodstream.

The Euthanasia Law was narrowly passed by the Northern Territory legislature but was bitterly opposed by Australia's leading medical association, Right to Life groups and the Roman Catholic Church. It was, in fact, repealed in 1997 due to their influence, making euthanasia once more illegal.

In his last letter, Dent stated that the Church had no right to influence laws on euthanasia.

The Humanist view

Humanists believe that people have the right to end their lives if that is their choice. They believe that death is the final event in life and that people have the right to die with dignity.

The Voluntary Euthanasia Society (EXIT)

This society was set up in 1935. Since then, it has campaigned to make it legal for a competent adult, who is suffering unbearably from an incurable illness, to die at their own considered request. Many of the members of VES are Humanists.

There is an Advance Directive form (also known as a Living Will) available from the Society, which expresses the person's wishes to his or her doctor, in the event of there being no reasonable prospect of a recovery. It says that, under certain circumstances, the patient does not want life prolonged by medical treatment, but that he or she does want to be kept comfortable with pain relief, even at the cost of shortening life. Advance Directives are held to be legally binding on doctors and are endorsed by the British Medical Association.

The case for legalisation

- A 1994 survey showed that over 10 per cent of doctors already help patients to die, despite the risk of prosecution.
- Nearly half of all doctors would be willing to help someone to die, if it were legal.
- 79 per cent of British people think this should be a legal choice.
- Medical advances mean that more people are living longer but dying of incurable diseases.
- Not everyone dies well. About 5 per cent of terminal pain is still uncontrollable, even in hospices.
- Everyone should have the choice of a dignified and peaceful death.

stop and think!

- The 'Deliverance Program' was alternatively described as the 'Death Machine'. 'Deliverance' and 'death' sound like opposites – what do you understand by them in this situation?

- In what situation, if any, would you agree to the use of the Deliverance Program by somebody in your family?

- Do you think the Church and other pro-life groups had a right to ban it? Why?

stop and think!

- What are some of the objections to the legalisation of euthanasia?

The hospice

A

> Accepting death's coming is the very opposite of doing nothing.
>
> *Dame Cicely Saunders*

The word 'hospice' comes from the Latin word 'hospes' meaning 'guest'. For thousands of years, the religious orders provided hospices where pilgrims and travellers could rest and eat, and where the sick were nursed.

What is a hospice?

- A hospice nowadays is a home for terminally ill patients. It can be purpose-built, or a wing within a hospital, but it is more than just a building. Hospice care also entails specially trained nurses visiting individuals in their homes.
- A hospice aims to relieve pain so that individuals can live their lives to the full.
- A hospice provides an open and safe atmosphere where patients are treated with respect and allowed to express their fears and anxieties.
- A hospice is as much about living as dying.

Origins

The modern movement started with a hospice established in Dublin by the Irish Sisters of Charity. In 1900, five of the Sisters came to the East End of London and, a few years later, set up St Joseph's Hospice in Hackney for those who were sick and could not afford to pay for care, or who were considered too disreputable for a hospital. About 60 years after this, Cicely Saunders, a young doctor, started working there and, as a result of her experiences, opened St Christopher's in Sydenham, Kent, in 1967 (**A**).

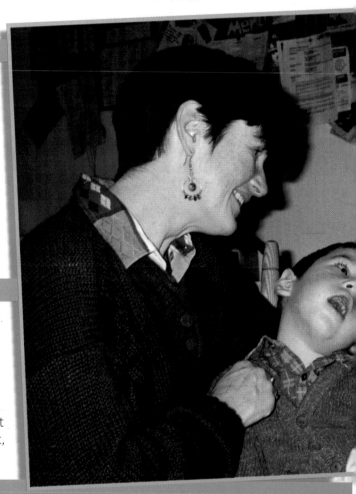

The patients

Some people need help to control the symptoms of their illness or disease. They will be given care, advice and support before returning home. Others, especially those who are living on their own, come in for a short break, to a place where all their needs are met and there are opportunities to socialise.

Whilst the hospice movement has become the expert in cancer care, they are also there for many other illnesses and diseases, including, more recently, **AIDS**.

Children are not usually cared for within the adult units. There are a few special hospices for them, such as Helen House in Oxford (**B**) and Zoë's Place baby hospice in Liverpool.

In all hospices the emphasis is on living. Some will organise candle-lit suppers or afternoon teas in the gardens. Then there are coach outings and trips to the local pub. Visitors are encouraged, and many come to teach a skill or to entertain. Friends and family can visit at almost any time of the day or night, and some visitors even bring the family pet in with them!

movement

When talking about visitors, Thelma Dalton, a day-care patient at a hospice, said 'I have often said that if they heard the laughter and the noise, they would never think they were walking into a hospice'.

B Helen House Hospice in Oxford

Funding

Over half the existing hospices have been built with independently raised funds through various charities. Although there is some NHS funding, it is not enough and more hospices are urgently needed.

A central principle in the teaching of all the world faiths is caring for people, particularly those disadvantaged by age, circumstances or illness.

Sikhism

The Sikh religion believes that God cares for everyone and considers caring as part of its religious heritage (**C**). Gurdwaras, or Sikh places of worship, often have medical clinics close by. Sikhs believe that the right relationship with God is based on prayer, work and charity. Service to the community (seva) entails all of these.

Islam

One of the Five Pillars of Islam is 'zakah', which expects all Muslims to give a proportion of their savings to charity. Further personal gifts to charity, known as 'sadaqah', are encouraged, but should be given discreetly and without show (**D**).

Buddhism

All Buddhists recognise the virtue of goodwill (metta) which involves compassion for others and generosity especially to those in need, such as the elderly and dying (**E**). Metta is regarded as a necessary rule of life, one which is essential to combat greed and selfishness.

C Sikh teaching

There can be no worship without performing good deeds... A place in God's court can only be attained if we do service to others in this world.

Adi Granth 4,26

D Muslim teaching

He may say [boastfully]: I have wasted vast riches. Does he think that none observes him? Have we not given him two eyes, a tongue and two lips and shown him the two paths (of right and wrong)? Yet he would not scale the height. Would that you know what the height is! It is the freeing of a bondsman [slave]; the feeding, in the day of famine, of an orphaned relation or a needy man in distress.

Qur'an surah 90:6–16

E Buddhist teaching

Let us fill our hearts with our own compassion – towards ourselves and towards all living beings. Let us pray that we ourselves cease to be the cause of suffering to each other. Let us plead with ourselves to live in a way which will not deprive other beings of air, water, food, shelter or the chance to live.

The Venerable Thich Nhat Hahn

QUESTIONS

1 What is the main difference between a hospice and a hospital?

2 What are the main aims of a hospice?

3 Why do you think many religious people support the work of the hospice movement?

4 What sort of qualities do people need when they work in a hospice?

Organ transplants

- In 1950, surgeons could not have transplanted a kidney.

- In 1994, an Englishman's life was saved because he had six organs transplanted into his body.

- At one time we would not have contemplated heart transplants because it was believed that the heart contained the soul.

- Today we are living with animal transplants.

Britain

A doctor in Cambridgeshire is genetically engineering pigs in an attempt to overcome the shortage of suitable organ donors. Transplants in America in the 1980s which involved killing primates for their organs led to an outcry, so now the research has transferred to pigs. A small amount of human DNA is introduced into the pig's ovum. Two of the pig's offspring are then mated to produce pigs with organs that will be accepted by the human body. **Insulin** from pigs is already being used in the control of human **diabetes**.

NHS Organ Donor Register

donorcard

I want to help others to live in the event of my death Please let your relatives know your wishes

A Do you think organs should be used automatically, unless the person has specifically requested otherwise?

France

On 28 July 1991, a 19-year-old boy, Christophe, suffered a fatal accident while riding his bike. The doctors could legally have taken his organs, but consulted his parents. They agreed, but with misgivings, to his heart, liver and kidneys being used. When they saw Christophe in the mortuary, his eyes had been taken as well. His distorted face is the most vivid picture that remains in his father's mind. The publicity which followed this led to a 20 per cent drop in organ donations, and to a change in the law in 1994. Now doctors have to seek permission even if there is a relevant donor card.

India

In poorer countries like India it is legal, at present, to buy a kidney. As medical evidence shows that healthy individuals can live a normal life span with one kidney and, as the average wage is around £5 a week, the £650 paid for a single kidney means there is no shortage of donors. However, media stories about the exploitation of the poor, and concern about the moral implications have led the government to propose a change in this law. Sadly, this is likely to lead to a black market in organ sales.

The USA

In April 1995, a pharmaceutical company took organs from pigs and put them into baboons. In Cleveland, Ohio, a leading neurosurgeon has successfully transplanted a monkey's head onto the body of another monkey. Although it could see, hear and taste, it could not move because of the damage to the spinal cord. In the near future, it should be possible to repair the nervous system.

A question that frequently arises when people are faced with the decision of whether to donate their organs or those of their loved ones is: 'Will my decision be compatible with my religious beliefs?' The majority of the world faiths, in fact, have little difficulty accepting the basic philosophy of transplant surgery. In theory, a religion such as Sikhism views the human body after death as a 'shell' because the 'atman' (spirit or soul) has left it (**B**).

In practice, however, and despite recognition of the need to have a constant supply of organs for surgery, many followers are reluctant to accept the idea of donating parts of the body. Many Muslims strongly believe that their body belongs to Allah, and so they are not in the position to donate any part of it. Supporting this view, in 1983 the Muslim Religious Council rejected organ donation by its followers, but has reversed this decision since then on condition that the donor consents in writing in advance. The Muslim Law Council issued a ruling in 1995 urging all Muslims to carry donor cards, and allowing the removal of essential organs after death (**C**). The organs of Muslim donors must, however, be transplanted immediately, and not stored in organ banks.

Judaism, like many of the other religions, teaches that saving a human life must take precedence over maintaining the 'sanctity' of the human body (**D**).

 B Sikh teaching

The dead may be cremated or buried, or thrown to the dogs, or cast into the waters or down an empty well. No one knows where the soul goes and disappears to.

Adi Granth 648

 C Muslim teaching

We have no policy against organ and tissue donation as long as it is done with respect for the deceased and for the benefit of the recipient.

Dr Abdel Rahma Osman, Director of the Muslim Community Center in Maryland, USA

 D Jewish teaching

If one is in the position to donate an organ to save another's life, it is obligatory to do so, even if the donor never knows who the beneficiary will be. The basic principle of Jewish ethics – 'the infinite worth of the human being' – also includes donation of corneas, since eyesight restoration is considered a life-saving operation.

Dr Moses Tendler, Chairman of the Bioethics Commission of the Rabbinical Council of America

stop and think!

- What are the advantages of having a donor card?
- What would be your feelings if you knew that, after your death, organs from your body would be used to save another's life or improve the quality of their life?
- How would you feel if the organs of one of your family were used?

QUESTIONS

1 Should we allow scientists complete freedom, or should there be clear internationally agreed guidelines to limit what they can do?

2 How do you feel about transplanting animal organs into human beings?

3 What will happen when we can, in theory, get a new body to replace the old worn-out one?

4 Animal rights activists say that we should not allow animal suffering caused through genetic experimentation. What do you think?

5 Will humans with animal transplants cease to be humans?

1 In your opinion, should medicine be looking to preserve life or improve life?

2 Can you think of ways that medicine has given us control over:
 a birth?
 b life?
 c death?

3 What is meant by the 'sanctity of life'?

4 Outline the current legal position in Britain regarding abortion.

5 In what situations do you think a Muslim or a Hindu might consider abortion to be acceptable?

6 Try and explain, in your own words, why the Roman Catholic Church opposes abortion.

7 Briefly explain the views on abortion held by the organisations Life and BPAS. Overall, which group do you think has the strongest case?

8 'It is a woman's right to choose whether to have an abortion or not.' Do you think anyone else should be involved in the decision?

9 Apart from abortion, what other options are available to a woman who has an unwanted pregnancy?

10 Why is the issue of adoption problematic for:
 a Muslims?
 b Hindus?

11 Explain the following words or terms:
 a IVF
 b AID
 c eugenics
 d cloning
 e ectogenesis

12 What are Cardinal Hume's main objections to gene therapy?

13 Why do you think the Roman Catholic Church opposes AID?

14 Describe in detail two different methods used to help overcome infertility.

15 Do you think human embryos should be used for medical research?

16 Some religious groups oppose reproductive engineering. What are their objections?

17 What is meant by surrogate motherhood, and why are some people opposed to it?

18 Name and describe in detail two ways (apart from surrogacy) in which modern science is helping couples who cannot have children naturally.

19 Describe how it is possible to have five 'parents'.

20 What does the word 'euthanasia' mean?

21 What developments have caused the euthanasia issue to be such a problem today, compared with 20 years ago?

22 Explain the following words or terms:
 a EXIT
 b hospice
 c living will

23 What is the teaching of one religion other than Christianity on euthanasia?

24 Is there a difference between 'being alive' and 'living'? Give reasons for your answer.

25 Which do you think are the best arguments against euthanasia?

26 Why is a human being allowed to live in a state where we would have no hesitation in putting an animal to sleep? Should we treat humans in the same way as we treat animals?

27 Why do you think some people are so keen to preserve their lives as long as possible, no matter how much pain they are in?

28 The Sikh view is that death is only a step towards another life. Does this belief have any bearing on the issue of euthanasia? Give reasons for your answer.

29 In what ways might an individual's attitude to euthanasia be different depending on the religious faith he or she held?

30 What do you think are the three most important features of hospice care?

31 Try and explain in your own words the Jewish attitude to the issue of organ transplants.

32 Why do Sikhs allow their organs to be used for transplants? Do you think they permit their bodies to be used for medical research?

33 Transplants cost a great deal of time and money. Do you think that the time, effort and resources used in these kinds of treatments and research could be better used in other ways? Give your reasons.

34 Muslims believe that all bodies belong to Allah and therefore individuals have no say in what happens to them after death. Do you think that this belief has any bearing on the issue of organ donation?

Introduction
One world

Unit aims

The aims of this unit are to present a range of environmental issues for you to consider and respond to. It also introduces you to some of the traditional religious beliefs relating to the care of planet earth and the advice given in teachings which are concerned about the use of the Earth and its resources.

Key concepts

From space, the planet Earth looks fine: white swirls of cloud moving over continents or the great oceans. Earth might look peaceful from such a distance but this is not the case. Some see the planet as something which exists purely for their convenience; others, however, care deeply about threats to the environment. The major world faiths find themselves in the difficult position of, accepting that we live in a technological world but, at the same time, urging restraint and conservation.

What is this unit about?

Some religions stand accused of allowing the environment to be slowly destroyed: after all, within Christianity and Judaism there is an assumption that the human race was appointed by God to be in control of nature. Other religions, such as Buddhism, insist that instead of being superior, we should be in close harmony – part of nature. This unit investigates and assesses the social pressures and religious teachings or matters concerning our survivial as a planet – exploitation and pollution, conservation and recycling. It also examines our attitudes towards the wildlife and nature that share this planet with us.

The last twenty years have witnessed green open spaces disappearing into housing and business projects, road systems and shopping malls. Along with so called 'progress' has come the destruction of this wildlife and nature with little thought for the future. Religious leaders recognise that the earth is at risk and urge their followers to do something about it

ONE WORLD
4
WONDERFUL WORLD?

wonderful world?

We also contribute to polluting the atmosphere, to fouling the seas and shorelines, and to contaminating the land with poisons. Nearly all the religious teachings are quite clear on these issues: it is essential that the correct balance is achieved between progress and conservation. At the moment, the price we are paying for progress is just too high. The Earth must be saved from further destruction otherwise future generations will inherit nothing.

It is ironic that we get excited about the possibility of life on other planets and yet we stand back and allow wholesale destruction of numerous species of plants and animals on this one. Some religions do not appear to take animal suffering seriously, whereas others are totally committed to preserving all types of life. The conclusion must be drawn that some religious believers must share a heavy responsibility for the continuing abuse of animals in the modern world. In *Mountain Lion*, D.H. Lawrence wrote in 1923, 'Man! The only animal in the world to fear.'

Losing life

Questions about pollution and conservation are becoming increasingly important to many people. These days, we are more aware of the consequences of our actions with regard to the health of our planet and all its living forms. People are prepared to act to ensure that the Earth has a future, but even so, large numbers of once common plants, fruit and vegetables are becoming extinct every year.

Many of our environmental problems are due to greed – to people's desire to make money. If you can produce, in a laboratory, a type of apple or carrot that is ready earlier, that lasts longer and that looks nicer, this will be the one growers and supermarket chains will want to sell (**A**). Everyone will make more profit. The destruction of the hedgerows, local beauty spots, the rainforests and other huge areas of land are often largely related to man's desire to make a profit. Land is also taken to provide housing and roads connecting towns and villages.

A In the last century, we have lost over 6,000 varieties of the precious apple

The saying 'apple of my eye' comes from the Bible and means 'child of my eye'. It is therefore precious and a symbol of God's love for human beings.

C

The world's religions have done virtually nothing to help physically save the world, or to place on the central agenda of their believers the need to care for or with nature.

Believing in the Environment, *Martin Palmer, from* World Goodwill Occasional Paper, 1988

D Christian teaching

The Lord took man and put him in the Garden of Eden to work it and take care of it.

Genesis 2:15

B The harmful effects of acid rain

Christianity

Some people believe that the major world faiths have not done enough to prevent this wide-scale destruction (**C**).

The signs today are more optimistic. Christians, for example, accept that they have certain responsibilities towards all living things because they believe that God placed them in the position of **stewards** for his creation (**D**). The problem is that many individuals believe that this stewardship allows them to exploit nature and behave irresponsibly, if they so wish.

The Catholic Agency For Overseas Development (CAFOD) and Christian Aid, recognising that the needs of people relate to a healthy local environment, have implemented tree planting schemes, and have worked to save local habitats.

Islam

Muslims believe that Allah created the world and everything in it. Human beings are the most important creation and have been given the role of 'guardians' (khalifah). They must look after the environment and ensure that it is never spoiled (**E**).

Buddhism

Buddhists believe that all individuals must actively try to protect the environment and ensure that any acts of neglect or destruction do not occur. The Buddhist view is to avoid harm to any living thing, from the largest mammal to the smallest insect (**F**).

 E Muslim teaching

Nature and the world are a field of exploration and the object of enjoyment for the Muslim. But whether he uses them for utility or for sheer enjoyment, he must avoid waste and excess. As a responsible agent of God and a conscientious trustee, he must always be mindful of others who share the world with him and who will succeed him in the future.

Islam in Focus,
by Hammudah Abdalati, 1981

stop and **think!**

- How long has your house, school or local leisure centre existed?
- What was your local area like 20, 50 or 100 years ago?
- We have lost 97 per cent of the varieties of vegetables that existed at the beginning of this century. Why do you think this is?
- Why are scientists rushing to endangered rainforests to take samples of some of the rare plants that exist only in these areas?
- How does the Bible support the belief that Christians are the stewards of all living things?
- Does the future survival of human beings depend on the survival of their environment?

 F Buddhist teaching

Monks and nuns may not 'destroy any plant or tree'.
Vinaya Pitaka

QUESTIONS

1 Read **E**.
  a What does 'conscientious trustee' mean?
  b Why should a conscientious trustee be concerned about endangered species?

2 How practical would it be if we all tried to follow the teaching in **F**?

3 Science fiction often shows food in the form of pills. If we allowed scientists to decide on the best foods to grow, how many plants, vegetables, fruits and trees would we lose forever?

4 What would you lose if a new hospital or supermarket was built in your area, or if a road was widened near you?

5 What advice do the religious teachings give us about how we should be looking after the planet Earth?

Poisoned planet

Pollution is not a new problem. For hundreds of years we have been aware of the devastating effects of smoke in the atmosphere. However, we seem to have ignored the lessons of history, and today, smoke is only one of the many ways in which we are poisoning the planet.

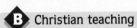

A Litter is just another way that we pollute our environment – can you think of any others?

The air is constantly fouled by the burning of fossil fuels in homes, cars, factories and power stations. Sulphur dioxide is released into the atmosphere and then washed back down in acid rain. The amount of carbon dioxide in the Earth's atmosphere has steadily risen leading to changes in the world's climates. The ozone layer, which protects us from harmful ultraviolet rays from the sun, is being eroded. This is caused by, among other things, the gases (known as CFCs) used in some aerosols, and in the exhausts of high-flying aircraft.

As well as the atmosphere, pollution also damages soil, rivers and seas. Around 70 per cent of the earth's surface is water and, in recent years, huge areas have been polluted by oil spillages, sewage and even toxic waste. When the supertanker, the *Exxon Valdez*, was involved in an accident off the Alaskan coast in 1989, over 50 million litres of oil were leaked into the sea. Beaches were covered in oil, thousands of animals died, and fishing stocks were severely affected for years.

Despite warnings from scientists that the tropical rainforests are irreplaceable and are the richest source of life on earth, they are felled at an alarming rate to provide us with fuel, timber, paper and land for farming. In addition, the mass clearing and burning of the forests contributes to air pollution and affects worldwide rainfall patterns. The land itself is threatened when it loses its tree cover. A desert may be all that remains where forests once grew.

B Christian teaching

We have no liberty to do what we like with our natural environment; it is not ours to treat as we please. 'Dominion' is not a synonym for 'domination', let alone 'destruction'.
The Rev Dr John Stott, President of Tear Fund

It is tragic that our technological mastery is greater than our wisdom about ourselves.
Pope John Paul II

We have no right to plunder, pollute, exploit, destroy, kill or in any way disrespect God's creation.
Resurgence, *Simon Phipps, Bishop of Lincoln, November, 1986.*

Christianity

All the major world religions speak about the need to respect the Earth and some, such as Christianity, Judaism and Islam, strongly believe that humankind has been appointed by God to be in command of nature. Since God is the creator of the world and has given human beings the responsibility for it, Christians have an extremely powerful reason to adopt a sensitive and caring policy towards nature, the environment and fellow creatures (**B**).

Hinduism

Hindus suggest that we are part of the natural world and humankind should be in harmony with it, rather than in control (**C**).

Sikhism

Sikh teachings insist that all followers should make every effort to help slow down and halt the present destructive trends in society (**D**).

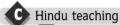

C Hindu teaching

Thou [Krishna – the Supreme Reality/Lord] art the dark blue butterfly, and the green parrot with red eyes. Thou art the thundercloud, the seasons and the oceans.

Shvetashvatara Upanishad, 4.4

The Isa Upanishad tells us that everything, from a blade of grass to the whole cosmos, is the home of God. God lives in every corner of existence. Therefore the whole creation is sacred.

Ranchor Prime, Hinduism and Ecology

D Sikh teaching

Sikhism teaches both respect and responsibility towards God's creation and the needs of future generations.

Indarjit Singh JP, Editor, Sikh Messenger

The Lord pervades all created beings; God creates all and assigns all their tasks.
Adi Granth 434

By God's will the Lord has created the creation and watches over all.
Adi Granth 1036

GREENPEACE

E Greenpeace members protesting against the dumping of Shell's 'Brent Spar' oil platform in the North Sea

Greenpeace, an organisation that has actively campaigned against the poisoning of the Earth, was founded in 1971 by Jim Bohlen, Paul Cote and Irving Stowe as a direct protest against the testing of H-bombs in the South Pacific. Irving Stowe introduced Bohlen to the Quakers who believe in a form of protest known as 'bearing witness'. This is a form of passive resistance that involves going to the scene of an activity you object to, and registering opposition to it simply by your presence there. Since 1971, Greenpeace volunteers have carried the symbols of ecology and peace to all corners of the Earth bearing witness to the pollution and the unnecessary destruction of many forms of life.

stop and think!

- In what ways has Greenpeace continued to 'bear witness'?

- Might a person's religious beliefs prevent involvement with an organisation like Greenpeace?

- What do you feel strongly enough about to want to 'bear witness'?

QUESTIONS

1 In what ways are we poisoning the planet?

2 Was Pope John Paul II right when he said that we do not have the wisdom to match our technological abilities?

3 'One of the UK's largest and longest-running schemes for monitoring the effects of acid rain may be discontinued following a threat by the Department of Environment to remove funding… The news comes as more evidence of the **detrimental** effects of acid rain on wildlife is surfacing.' *BBC Wildlife Magazine, Vol 14. No. 4.* What is your immediate reaction to this extract?

4 Conservation

A Copper mine in Peru

B A bottle bank

C Fishing for sand eels in the North Sea

The Earth has been around for a very long time: 4,600 million years at the last estimate! For most of that time, it has been very different from the world we live in today. Modern technology demands materials from the Earth's crust, but the enormous progress that technology has made has come at a cost. Human beings and other species have suffered and even been destroyed. Conservation means to preserve what we want and need, and to save some of the things we use and enjoy for future generations.

There are over four billion people on the planet and we are consuming the Earth's resources at an alarming rate. There is no guarantee that the Earth has a long-term future. We now recognise that there is an urgent need for conservation.

In September 1986, leaders of all six major world religions met for the 25th anniversary of the World Wide Fund for Nature. The conference took place in Assisi, Italy, a place chosen in recognition of the work of St Francis of Assisi. For centuries, his teachings on conservation and ecology have been widely admired, and in Christian circles he is acknowledged as the patron saint of animals.

All the main religious traditions acknowledged that drastic steps must be taken to curb this devastation. Father Lanfranco Serrini spoke for all the representatives when he stated: 'We members of major world religions and traditions… are gathered here… to awaken all people to their historical responsibility for the welfare of Planet Earth.'

stop and think!

Look at the above photos.

- How can we help to preserve the planet's resources?

- In what ways can we contribute to conservation?

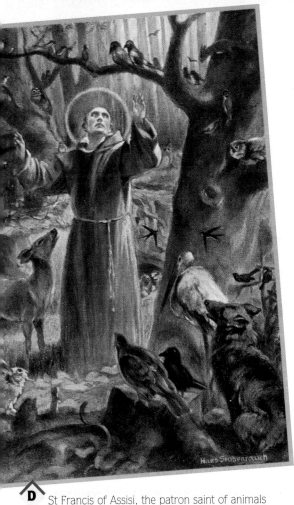

D St Francis of Assisi, the patron saint of animals

All world religions urge the need to recognise that the Earth and its resources should not be abused in any way (**E**, **F** and **G**).

Just as St Francis is recognised as the 'green' saint, Buddhism has always been concerned with the issues of conservation and preserving the natural things on earth. This is hardly surprising, given that the principle of 'ahimsa' (harmlessness) dominates Buddhist thought (**E**).

 E Buddhist teaching

Our ancestors viewed the Earth as rich and bountiful, which it is. Many people in the past saw nature as inexhaustibly sustainable, which we now know is the case only if we care for it. It is not difficult to forgive destruction in the past which resulted from ignorance. Today, however, we have access to more information, and it is essential that we re-examine ethically what we have inherited, what we are responsible for and what we will pass on to coming generations.

His Holiness Tenzin Gyatso, the 14th Dalai Lama

F Christian teaching

For centuries, far too many Christians have presumed that God's love is primarily directed at them, and that His natural order was created mainly for the use – and abuse – of humankind. Today, such a man-centred attitude to our fragile and exhausted planet is at last beginning to look not only selfish and parochial, but also irresponsible and potentially disastrous. We must realise that the way to maintain the value and preciousness of the human is by re-affirming the preciousness of the non-human also – of all that is.

The Right Reverend Lord Runcie, former Archbishop of Canterbury

G Muslim teaching

We are not masters of this earth; it does not belong to us to do what we wish. It belongs to God and He has entrusted us with its safekeeping... His trustees are responsible for maintaining the unity of His creation, the integrity of the earth, its flora and fauna, its wildlife and natural environment.

The Muslim Declaration at Assisi, 1986

Muslim teachings are quite clear about the responsibility followers have towards the planet and the creatures on it, and towards the use of natural resources. The balance of the planet is seen as essential, and all Muslims are urged to stop exploiting the Earth's resources and to conserve as much as possible (**G**).

QUESTIONS

Read **E**, **F** and **G** again.

1 What was the Assisi Declaration?

2 What kind of attitudes do the religious teachings encourage their followers to adopt? Can you find any difference of emphasis between the religions?

3 Which religious teaching do you think is the most powerful? Give reasons for your answer.

4 Explain how people should act 'with responsibility for the welfare of Planet Earth'.

ONE WORLD
4
WONDERFUL WORLD?

Animal rights and wrongs

A Protesting against live animal exports

stop and think!

- Is there a difference between nature being responsible for the extinction of a type of animal, and human beings being responsible?

- Which animals are 'hunted', and which of these animals has an active protest group campaigning on its behalf?

Medical experimentation

Food   Fur

Cosmetic experimentation

Hunting and entertainment

B Animal rights?

Young people are often very concerned about animal rights issues. Many not only voice their concerns but are actively involved in local and national protests (A). In this century, we have made real progress in our awareness of some of the problems facing the animal world, but are our actions based on understanding and knowledge or are they purely emotional?

In the last few centuries – equal to a few seconds in the life of the planet – we have lost hundreds of thousands of unique and beautiful birds and animals. Hundreds more, including the humpback whale, the white rhinoceros and the Siberian tiger are on the lists of endangered species.

There are many reasons for the loss of these species. Changes to the natural habitat, excessive hunting and fishing, pollution and ignorance have all contributed to the extinction of many species.

Without doubt, human beings have been responsible for hunting animals to the verge of extinction from the very beginnings of their history, but some animals that could not adapt to changes in their environment disappeared naturally. The scientist, Charles Darwin, called this 'natural selection' – the survival of the fittest. What Darwin could not have foreseen when he published his theories in 1859, was the speed with which human beings would set about changing their environment. Quite often, animals were unable to cope with such sudden changes.

Since the 1960s, there has been considerable debate about farming methods. Whilst there has been some move from **battery farming** to **free range**, change is very slow. The main reason that animals are still kept in unhealthily cramped conditions, is that not everyone is prepared to pay the extra cost of eggs and meat. Many people these days, especially teenagers, are changing to a **vegan** or **vegetarian** diet. The numbers are increasing each year, but still form only a small percentage of the population.

All the world religions profess concerns about the way animals are poorly treated. They focus attention on five general controversial areas (**B**).

84

Christianity

The vast majority of Christians acknowledge that animals are simply different creatures from humans, part of God's creation and deserving of respect (**C**).

Islam

Islam lays great emphasis on animal welfare and the responsibility of all humans to show compassion and to look after other creatures. There are many verses in the Qur'an concerning the issue of animal welfare, and the guidelines are quite clear (**D**).

Buddhism

Buddhism has a greater concern for the welfare of animals than any other world religion. The teachings make it very clear that no living thing should be harmed: for Buddhists, this teaching is radical and far-reaching (**E**).

An MP, Richard Martin, was laughed out of a session of Parliament when he proposed a Bill in 1821 to prevent cruelty to horses. This attitude did not stop the law being passed in 1822, or Martin, William Wilberforce MP and a London vicar, Arthur Broom, from founding the Royal Society for the Prevention of Cruelty to Animals in 1824. The RSPCA has since been in the forefront of campaigns for new laws protecting both domesticated and wild animals in Britain.

The book *Animal Liberation* had a real impact because its author, Peter Singer, was not an animal activist but a philosopher. He argued that because animals suffered, and acted, in similar ways to humans then animals should have the same rights as humans.

In 1993 Peter Singer, with other phiosophers, scientists, and writers set out a 'Declaration on Great Apes', the campaign being called 'The Great Ape Project'.

This argued that it is wrong to imprison, kill or cause pain to any of the great apes. It also argued that apes must be regarded as persons rather than property. This has serious consequences for zoos, laboratories, advertising agencies, television and film companies.

C Christian teaching

And God said, 'Let the water teem with living creatures, and let birds fly above the earth across the expanse of the sky.' So God created the great creatures of the sea and every living and moving thing with which the water teems, according to their kinds, and every winged bird according to its kind. And God saw that it was good. God blessed them and said, 'Be fruitful and increase in number and fill the water in the seas, and let the birds increase on the earth.'

Genesis 1:20–22

… O Lord, you preserve both man and beast.

Psalm 36:6

D Muslim teaching

One day, the Prophet passed by a camel which was so thin that its back had shrunk to its belly. He said, 'Fear Allah in these beasts – ride them in good health and free them from work while they are still in good health.' The Prophet said, 'It is a great sin for man to imprison those animals which are in his power.'

The Muslim Educational Trust, Animal Welfare

E Buddhist teaching

Whosoever in this world destroys life… such a one interferes with their own progress in this very world.

The Dhammapada 246–7

I will avoid taking life. I will try to show loving kindness towards all creatures.

From the Five Precepts

However mean, however small, the animal may seem, life to that animal is as important and precious as it is to us.

Worlds of Faith, by John Bowker, Ariel Books, 1983

Do humans need animals more than animals need humans? **F**

QUESTIONS

1 In **D**, what does the Prophet regard as a great sin?

2 Why would you expect a Buddhist to be actively involved in saving endangered animals?

3 Who do you think are more important: animals or humans? Why?

Why worry?

When we look around us we see many examples of the beauty of our natural environment. It does not seem to matter where you live – there are always places that are capable of inspiring us to feel our planet is special. So, what is the problem? Why are so many people concerned about the future of our wonderful world?

A Ajahn Pongsak at work in a Thai forest

B These villagers in Zimbabwe built this dam themselves with the help of Christian Care. The water will be used to irrigate their fields.

There are hundreds of organisations which encourage millions of individuals to involve themselves actively in environmental issues. The Worldwide Fund for Nature and Friends of the Earth, for example, are both important in influencing public awareness of environmental concerns throughout the world.

Every country has people who campaign about issues that affect the country they live in and issues that affect the whole world. Ajahn Pongsak, a Buddhist monk in Thailand, is trying to educate people in his country about the importance of replanting trees after more than 50 per cent of the country's forests disappeared in only 30 years.

International conferences are frequently held where environmental issues are discussed, and attempts to find solutions are made. In recent years organisations have started to join forces to tackle some of the problems that worry them most.

In the UK, another result of concerns for the local environment was the establishment of the Church and Conservation Project in 1987. Supported by the World Wildlife Fund, the Royal Agricultural Society and the Nature Conservancy Council, this project assists with the training of clergy in rural areas, and gives advice on the best ways to conserve the land holdings of the Churches. Particularly effective has been the Living Churchyard Project, which has identified burial grounds as actual and potential havens for wildlife.

stop and think!

- **What kinds of problems are causing people to worry about the future of the world?**

- **Which environmental problems worry you most?**

- **Why do so many people feel so strongly about the environment that they are prepared to do more than just complain?**

- **Do you or does anyone you know belong to an organisation concerned with the environment?**

Whilst it is true that governments and large companies are more likely to take notice of large groups than of individuals, there are people, as we have seen, who have made a significant contribution to the environment on their own. It should also be remembered that most of the large organisations concerned with environmental issues were started by individuals prepared to act on their beliefs and ideals.

Islam

Islamic teachings make clear that Allah entrusted the planet to mankind, and it is important that Muslims play a leading part in the efforts to protect the environment (**D**).

C The United Nations (UN) 'Earth Summit' in 1992

Christianity

Similar sentiments are expressed within the Christian community, which is increasingly concerned with the 'environmental crisis'. It is up to the Churches, to new movements, and to leaders to take the initiative (**E**).

D Muslim teaching

It is Allah who has subjected the sea to you... And he has subjected to you, as from Him, all that is in the heavens and on earth.

Qur'an surah 45:12–13

E Christian teaching

Nature now belongs to us and is part of us, so that our whole life is interwoven with it... We want to be human in the world, rather than human by conquering it.

Towards a Green Humanism, *Don Cupitt, General Studies Review Vol. 1 No 1.*

Buddhism

A very important part of Buddhist teaching is focused on the interaction between mankind and the environment. We are part of the natural world and we should be attempting to preserve it. At the same time, Buddhists are aware of the need to live in the modern world, making use of resources of raw materials and fuel (**F**).

F Buddhist teaching

(Buddhism) attaches great importance to wildlife and the protection of the environment on which every being in the world depends for survival.

The Assisi Declaration, 29 September 1986

QUESTIONS

1 What advantages are there for the environment if more organisations work together on one particular problem or issue?

2 What do pictures **A**, **B** and **C** tell us about the commitment some people are prepared to make because of their concerns about the environment?

3 If individuals and organisations around the world are working to save the environment, why are there still real worries about the future of this planet?

4 'What befalls the earth befalls all the sons and daughters of the earth... This we all know: All things are connected like the blood that unites us. We did not weave the web of life, we are merely a strand in it. Whatever we do to the web, we do to ourselves.' (*Brother Eagle, Sister Sky*: A Message from Chief Seattle, by Susan Jeffers, Puffin Books, 1993)

What should we be doing to ensure that we stop losing the varied life of this planet?

1 Briefly describe what the following words mean:

  a extinct

  b steward

  c CAFOD

  d conscientious trustee

  e pollution

  f natural selection

  g Assisi Declaration

2 Name two organisations committed to environmental issues.

3 Look back at the five areas where animals are exploited. Are any of these acceptable? Give reasons for your answers.

4 Explain some of the religious reasons why people should be concerned about the dangers to the environment.

5 Describe and explain how Christian teachings might affect our attitudes in caring for the environment.

6 Describe the Christian teachings and the teachings of one other religion on stewardship and creation. Discuss whether you think this is a good way to think about our responsibilities.

7 'It's worth putting up with a few environmental problems if people can be given jobs and earn a salary.' How do you think religious people might respond to this comment? In your answer, try and look at different points of view.

8 Explain religious attitudes concerning the acceptability of eating meat and using products tested on animals.

9 Read this extract from a Greenpeace publication.

> Think of the planet Earth as a 46-year-old.
>
> The Earth is thought to be around 4,600 million years old, an almost inconceivable timespan. For the moment, think of it as someone in middle age, 46 years old.
>
> This person is a late developer. Nothing at all is known about their first seven years and only sketchy information exists about the next 35 years. It is only at the age of 42 that the earth began to flower.
>
> Dinosaurs and the great reptiles did not appear until a year ago, when this planet reached 45. Mammals arrived only eight months ago. In the middle of last week, human-like apes evolved into ape-like humans, and at the weekend the last ice age enveloped the Earth.
>
> Modern humans have been around for four hours. During the last hour, we discovered agriculture. The industrial revolution began just a minute ago. During those sixty seconds of biological time, humans have made a rubbish tip of Paradise.
>
> We have caused the extinction of many hundreds of species of animals, many of which have been here longer than us, and ransacked the planet for fuel. Now we stand like brutish infants, gloating over this meteoric rise to ascendancy, poised on the brink of the final mass extinction and of effectively destroying this oasis of life in the solar system.

What is your reaction to this article?

10 Describe the example of the Prophet Muhammad concerning responsibility to animals.

11 What difficulties are there in following Buddhist principles in the world today?

12 'God made the Earth so he should look after it.' Do you agree? Give reasons to support your answer and show that you have considered different points of view.

Introduction
One world

Unit aims

There are two main aims of this unit: to consider how religion is portrayed in the media and the arts, and how it contributes to these; also to consider how the world's religions affect the community at local and worldwide levels, with special attention given to their role in caring for the disadvantaged. You will also learn how to compose a questionnaire in order to find out information about a community for yourself.

Key concepts

The major world religions have made enormous contributions to the areas of art, literature and music. Almost all western art and sculpture until the Middle Ages had religion as its subject, and many of the greatest musical works ever written were religious in inspiration. Islam has given us the most beautiful **calligraphy** and design, and religious architecture is some of the most impressive in the world.

The modern-day media in all of their many forms have had an impact on the modernisation of many religious ideas and, in turn, have been influenced by the different faiths. Religions are less suspicious of the media nowadays and, similarly, the media are learning to take more care instead of making sweeping generalisations. A healthy respect between the religious and the **secular** is now beginning to exist.

Large and small communities all over the world have been influenced by the different faiths, which have sought to improve the lot of the poor and disadvantaged. Where the State cannot help, religious groups and charities do their best to care for people in need.

many religions

What is this unit about?

Within this unit, you will find images of religion portrayed in a variety of media such as television, newspapers, film and the internet, and you will see how religious ideas have permeated nearly evryr part of our lives. You will see, too, how society is gradually becoming more tolerant of 'foreign' ideas and attitudes.

This unit also shows the work of charitable religious groups such as Muslim Aid, which has poured millions of pounds of aid into the poorer countries of the world.

ONE WORLD
5
MANY RELIGIONS

Baroness Margaret Thatcher (Prime Minister of the UK 1979–90) was reported to have once said that people were only individuals, and not part of a bigger group (**A**). Yet, much earlier, the poet, John Donne, pointed out that no one can be completely alone (**B**).

A

There is no such thing as a community, only a group of individuals.
Margaret Thatcher

B

No man is an island, entire of itself. Every man is a piece of the Continent, a part of the main.
John Donne, 1573–1631, Devotions XVII

stop and **think!**

- What do you think about Baroness Thatcher's statement? How do you think her statement would be viewed by: a politician? a minister of the church? a housewife? an elderly person? a shopkeeper?

- What do you think John Donne meant by 'entire of itself?'

stop and **think!**

- Which 'communities' do you belong to? Do some of your answers surprise you?

People belong to many different types of groupings or 'communities', some more formalised than others. For example, people can belong to the community of the school, or the work place, the community of the local area in which they live, or the 'faith' community.

Communities vary considerably depending on what draws them together. You can choose to belong to a particular group, but there is less choice about who becomes your neighbour.

Some communities are linked to others that share the same faith or ideals as themselves. However, it is important to note that there can be different opinions and ideas even within the same community. Much will depend on what people consider to be the 'authority' behind their beliefs and attitudes.

Areas which can cause problems in the workplace, in schools and in the wider community, are the observance of religious holy days and festivals, specific laws and practices. Fortunately, in our communities we now accept the need to recognise such events, and there is evidence of far greater tolerance on all sides. Religions, too, have adapted as far as they can, emphasising that they must respect and keep the laws of the country in which they are living.

the community

Islam

The vast majority of Muslims are actively involved in their community. However, living in a country where most of the population do not share the same religious beliefs can be a challenge. It is not always easy to keep the beliefs, values and traditions of your religion if they bring you into conflict with the wider community (**C**).

 C Muslim teaching

Employers should show sensitivity towards their employees and ensure that they are able to take leave on these days, as they form an integral part of their religious practices.

The Muslim Educational Trust

Buddhism

Many religious leaders have pointed out that it is not easy to have a firm religious conviction and yet to be tolerant of those whose views are different from one's own. Buddhists have achieved this kind of tolerance to a large exent, although many do not find it easy to live within a society whose aims are particularly materialistic (**D**).

 D Buddhist teaching

The Western way of life and Buddhism I don't think mix terribly well together. We are far too materialistic – I am far too materialistic. I spend all my time at work, wondering how to get more money, and that does worry me, because I don't think you can live properly in the West and be a good Buddhist.

Worlds of Faith,
by John Bowker, Ariel Books, 1983

Christianity

In Britain, every village, town and city skyline appears to be dominated by church spires or towers. Although attendance in churches appears very low, there is little doubt that the Christian influence runs through every community. Most Christians believe it is their duty to be involved in their local communities, for example, organising charitable relief. They hope, as would any member of a religious tradition, that they offer a visible model of the way people can live in the community in more loving and just ways (**E**).

 E Christian teaching

Let no debt remain outstanding, except the continuing debt to love one another, for he who loves his fellow man has fulfilled the law... Let us behave decently...

Romans 13:8,13

93

Religion in the community

The public face of the community

People know who lives in your house because they see who goes in and out regularly. They may even know something about your circumstances by what you wear, for example, a school uniform or police uniform, or by the times you leave home and return, for example, as a shift worker. This is also true at a place of worship, which will be the centre or 'home' of a particular faith community.

stop and think!

- Think about the places of worship in your community. What makes you aware of them?

- What might give you clues about the regular activities that happen there?

QUESTIONS

To understand any place of worship, you need to watch what goes on and ask certain questions about what you see.

- Is there a notice-board outside?
- Do you notice that different ages or different genders attend at particular times?
- Do all those who attend dress similarly?
- Can you hear anything?
- Is the inside of the building always arranged in the same way?
- Are there particular rooms set aside for particular activities?

F A gurdwara, a place of worship for the Sikh community

What information can you find from this notice-board about the services that occur within this church?

A visit to a place of worship will answer a lot of these questions, but it needs to be well organised. It is important to think about:

- exactly what you want to know
- the questions you will ask to get this information
- the best person to show you round
- how you will record the information

There will be times when a place of worship becomes a hive of activity. Usually, there will be only be one main act of worship in a week, but there will also be weddings, funerals and christenings. In fact, some people only attend a place of worship for an important family event like this. These events tend to be more noticeable in the local community.

Festivals are also times when celebrations spill out into the local community or draw people in who might not usually attend.

QUESTIONS

1 Choose a local area you know and draw a sketch map of it, like the one here. Mark on it:
   a any well-known local landmarks
   b any local amenities e.g. library
   c any places of worship

2 What good things can you conclude about the neighbourhood you have considered?

3 What do you think might be missing from the community? How could you make any improvements?

4 Which festivals are celebrated in the places. How are they celebrated?

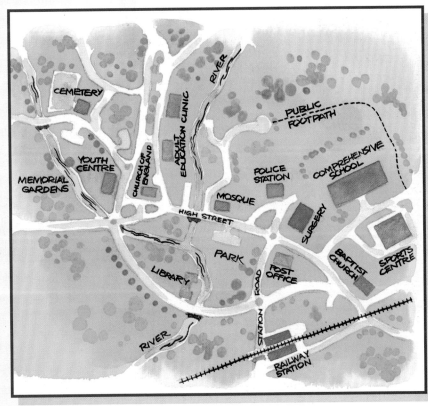

Designing a questionnaire

This section gives information on designing and using a questionnaire.

The principles behind designing a questionnaire are the same whether you intend to fill it in yourself or give it to someone else to complete. (The second way is likely to give the most accurate responses.)

The style of the questions is all important. It depends very much on what you hope to achieve from the answers and how you intend to use them.

Questionnaires are most often used when a newspaper, TV channel or market research organisation wants to interview a large number of people to gain a view of general feelings on an issue.

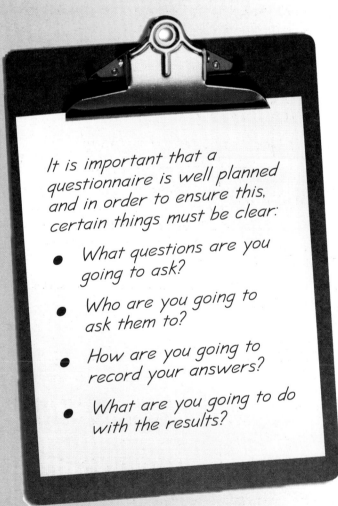

It is important that a questionnaire is well planned and in order to ensure this, certain things must be clear:

- What questions are you going to ask?
- Who are you going to ask them to?
- How are you going to record your answers?
- What are you going to do with the results?

The questions

There are many different sorts of questions that you could ask:

- Questions that classify people (e.g. by age, gender, occupation, etc). These are only worth asking if any of these things would make a difference to your conclusions. Record answers in boxes.
- Questions that will give you facts – useful if you want to know 'how often' or 'how much'.
- Questions that will show you how much people know about something – useful for finding out exact knowledge.
- Questions that seek an opinion – useful for advertising or for gaining support to change something.
- Questions that find out why a person does or does not do something – again, good for suggesting change.

It is important to understand the difference between open and closed questions.

- Open: e.g. What do you think about the new church hall? – will give a lot of information, but are difficult to analyse because answers will be so varied. Best used in interviews to get people to expand on their views.
- Closed: e.g. Do you think the church should ever be locked? – will limit the answers given and so are easy to analyse by ticking boxes. Best used if tables or graphs are needed.

Problems to avoid

Try to avoid questions that are unclear or do not allow people to say what they really think:

- Leading questions: 'Don't you agree that…'
- Presuming questions: 'When did you…'; 'How many have you…'
- Double questions: 'Do you think that… and that…'
- Questions where the choice of answer is vague or unclear: 'regularly' or 'occasionally' may mean different things to different people.
- Questions which have difficult words or assume knowledge, for example, technical terms not understood by the majority of people.

Think of examples for each of these sorts of questions so that you are sure you understand.

The sample

Who will you ask your questions to? This group is the sample. The larger the sample, the more accurate the results, but remember, asking questions and analysing results is very time consuming:

- 50 is a good number, and is easy to percentage.
- 20 is the minimum, if the questionnaire is to be successful.

Be sure to select a random sample – a good cross section of people.

Recording the answers

It is important to find a clear way of recording the answers before you begin. The most common way is to ensure that your questionnaire has spaces in which people can write their answers. Or you may prefer to have a grid drawn up so that you can write down the answers they tell you. This grid would need spaces for:

- The name of the person being interviewed (or a number, if your sample is to remain anonymous)
- The number of each question that will be asked
- All the possible answers for each question.

Analysing the results

It is important to analyse your results carefully so that you can draw realistic and helpful conclusions. There are several ways of representing your findings:

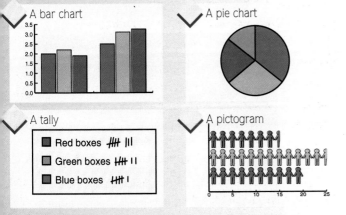

A bar chart   A pie chart

A tally   A pictogram

Red boxes 卌 |||
Green boxes 卌 ||
Blue boxes 卌 |

The method of analysing the results you choose may depend on whether you asked closed or open questions.

What do you expect to find out?

Having completed your research and presented your findings, you are now ready to draw conclusions, so what sort of things should you be looking for? Some suggestions might be:

- Look for patterns emerging, e.g. answers that come up several times. Make a note of these.
- Does age or gender influence a person's response? Make a note of anything you find.
- Are there similarities or differences between the responses of people who belong to a religious group and those who do not? What might you conclude from this?
- Are there responses that suggest that a question was not a good choice? Make a note of these.

Can you think of other things to look for?

Writing up your findings

When you have analysed your research, look at what you have noted and summarise your main findings. Comment particularly on anything that surprised you. Be sure to note any problems you encountered, and any changes you would make if you did it again.

Finish your work with some assessment of how successful your research was.

Publishing your findings

How might your findings be presented in a way that would interest or be of help to others? Which of these things could you do?

- Design a booklet that could be used by a local community group to advertise itself and its activities.
- Record an audio or video tape that would be of interest to local radio or television.
- Produce a series of posters.
- Simply get involved in some local activities yourself!

Religion in ar

Throughout the history of humankind, art has been used to express beliefs, to worship, to teach and to inspire.

A A stained-glass window

B The ceiling of the chapel in Wurzburg, Germany

C An icon of Jesus and the Virgin Mary

Christianity

From the time of Constantine the Great, when Christianity was established as the state religion of the Roman Empire, art has been used to glorify God, to teach the faithful and to help to convert others to the Christian faith.

Early churches and cathedrals were built as a house of God with perfect **geometry,** because it was believed that the universe had been created by God according to certain mathematical rules.

Some of the most famous architecture, paintings and sculptures are to be found in places of Christian worship around the world (**A**, **B** and **C**).

Perhaps less well known are the numerous banners which play an important part in the worship of many Christians (**D**).

MATTHEW 4-19

D A Christian banner

stop and think!

- Why was it so important in the early history of the Christian Church for art to be used to tell people about the life and teachings of Jesus?

- Which of the pictures best expresses Christian beliefs, in your opinion?

Islam

Islamic art is very different from Christian, partly because it is forbidden to draw, paint or sculpt the human figure. This prohibition is because Muslims believe that any danger of **idolatry** should be avoided. Drawings or statues could easily become objects of worship. Instead, Muslims make use of geometric shapes and create elaborate patterns (**E**). Muslims believe that art glorifies Allah, celebrates creation and that artists should work through prayer.

One of the art forms that has always been important in Islamic countries is calligraphy. Muslims believe that 'calligraphy is the geometry of the spirit'. They also believe that writing any part of the Qur'an should be considered a religious experience.

E The most beautiful geometric art is often found in a mosque

Buddhism

In Buddhism, art plays an important part in expressing beliefs. This can be seen through the main forms of the Buddha (**F**), mandalas, and the Zen gardens.

 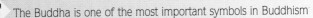 The Buddha is one of the most important symbols in Buddhism

QUESTIONS

1 Why does Islamic law forbid any image of the human figure?

2 'Art and religion are means to similar states of mind.' (Clive Bell, English art critic)

   a What do you think Clive Bell means?

   b In what ways do you agree or disagree with him?

Religion in music

With some exceptions, religious, or sacred, music is vocal music, but there is considerable variety within each of the main religious traditions.

A A Gospel choir – one of the many forms of Christian music

Christianity

In the Christian tradition, the earliest vocal music is the hymn. In the fifth century, 'hymn' was defined as a religious composition sung by a stationary chorus.

To begin with, the **Psalms** formed the basis for all hymns, and the early church decided that only hymns using the words of the scriptures were to be used during services.

As the Roman Catholic Church and the Church of England did not encourage the use of hymns, it was not until the eighteenth century that hymns became an important part of Christian worship. Isaac Watts and the Wesley brothers were responsible for writing some of the most powerful songs still used in Christian services.

There are approximately 950,000 Christian hymns in existence, although only a small number of these are in use today.

Gospel music as we know it had its roots in the American Negro spirituals. The 'Golden Age' of Gospel started in the 1920s and 1930s when Thomas Dorsey began composing songs based on familiar spirituals and hymns, mixed with blues and jazz rhythms. These brought a much needed message of hope to the churches during the depression in the USA.

One of the best known religious texts set to music is that of the *Passion*. This enacts the Passion of Jesus Christ during Holy Week. It is based on the old miracle and Passion plays which were semi-dramatic presentations of New Testament stories. J.S. Bach's The St Matthew's Passion is a fine example of this type of composition. One of the most famous Passion plays is performed every ten years at Oberammergau in Bavaria, Southern Germany.

Christian music today combines the traditional influence of the scriptures with every imaginable form of music (**A**).

Islam

Islam has extremes of belief in the importance, or otherwise, of music in religion.

The **Orthodox** tradition within Islam states that 'Islam has no music'. Yazid III, a noted Umayyad Caliph, warned, in AD 740, 'Beware of singing for it will steal your modesty, fill you with lust and ruin your virtue.'

Whilst the call to prayer is based on the Arabic scales used for all Arab music, it is not considered music. A court case in Cairo in 1977 decreed that the reciting of the Qur'an was an act of worship, and did not involve innovation. It follows therefore, to actually deliver the Qur'an through music is considered a sin.

However, as with all the main world religions, there is considerable variations of belief within Islam. **Sufism** is a mystical movement which moved away from the more traditional Muslim faith, and within this sub-sect, music plays an important part in worship. Religious poetry set to music, called **qawwali**, is used to arouse mystical love, central to the experience of Sufism.

Nowadays, Muslim youth around the world also sings to express its beliefs, as do all young people (**B**).

Judaism

The dispersion of the Jews has meant that very little traditional music has survived. It is believed that the **Yemenite** Jewish music is the nearest to the original ancient **Hebrew**. This ancient Jewish community is believed to date back to 585 BC. Vocal music such as the *Lamentations of Jeremiah* is believed to be closest to that belonging to the earliest Jews (**C**).

As progress marches on
People get so busy
That they forget their duty
To pray to God five times a day
They are so drunk with progress
They think the computer is God (you're kidding!)
When they talk about the world
They're wonderfully clever
But talk to them about religion
And suddenly they're allergic.

Rhoma Irama, 'Qur'an dan Koran' from 'Indonesian Popular Music 2', Smithsonian Folkways

B The lyrics of a popular Indonesian song

stop and think!

'Music recognises no religious differences – indeed it is something of a religion in its own right.' From *World Music: The Rough Guide*, Penguin, 1994

- **What role do you think music plays in religion?**

C Traditional Jewish musicians

QUESTIONS

1 'Music has always had its critics: just think about Rock and Roll in the fifties, The Beatles and The Rolling Stones in the sixties, Punk music in the seventies.' Why is music regarded by some people as dangerous?

2 Why do you think the Orthodox tradition within Islam is unhappy with any involvement in musical activities?

Religion in

A Some forms of the media

The word 'media' is a term used to describe different forms of communication. There are many ways to communicate within society – through newspapers and magazines, books, television, radio and the internet.

The media are part of our everyday lives, and as such, are all around us, and taken for granted. Quite often, we do not realise how much we are influenced by them, how powerful they are, and what effects they have on our lives. We need only look at how the media were manipulated and used to create hatred towards Jewish people in the 1930s and 1940s to realise how powerful they can be.

stop and think!

- How many types of 'media' can you see around you at the moment?

- Which form of media do you think is the most important? Why? Remember to consider which media forms are most easily available to people.

It is clear that the media exert enormous influence on us and are often criticised for various reasons. Major criticisms are that the media focus on negative aspects of life, that they are biased, and that they create and use stereotypes. No matter how hard the media try to show a true picture of society, they can never succeed.

Religion, in particular, appears to be a difficult area to cover and, all too often, while covering religious aspects of life, the media confirm prejudices by putting forward powerful images. Newspapers and television focus on 'sensational' stories such as religious hatreds, cults and scandals (**B**). These sell far more papers, than, for example, profiles of the work of Christian Aid or Muslim Aid.

the media

stop and think!

- What 'images' do these headlines give their readers?
- Is it fair to say that many of these headlines are more about politics than religion?

Having acknowledged the negative aspects of the media, it is also important to recognise that they play a very important role in religious life. Documentaries on individuals such as Mother Teresa and Bhagat Puran Singh often promote interest, concern and most importantly, greater tolerance.

Even where the issues are controversial, many will argue that it is a good thing for religions to be examined and to have a much higher profile. In recent years this has been seen in the area of sport. The spectacular refusal of the athlete Eric Liddell (featured in the film *Chariots of Fire*) to race on a Sunday was not an isolated event. Until 1960, Rule 25 of the Football Association stated that 'matches shall not be played on Sundays… A player shall not be compelled to play on Sundays… on Good Friday or Christmas Day.'

In the 1990s, a large number of sports personalities have been profiled in the media for their religious beliefs. For example, Mike Tyson, the ex-World Heavyweight Boxing champion who converted to Islam; and Michael Jones, one of the best All Black rugby players in New Zealand who refused to participate in sport on Sundays. Such individuals are often seen as 'role models' and their influence, particularly among young people, cannot be underestimated. By seizing on certain examples, the media highlight the difficulties faced by a believer trying to reconcile traditional items of belief with modern day standards.

For the Algerian, Hassiba Boulmerka, the 1992 World Champion and Olympic 1500 metres gold medallist, home became a no-go area. Her Muslim beliefs and values clashed with her commitment to sport. In an interview she stated: 'You cannot wear the **hajib** in the stadium, just as you cannot wear shorts in the mosques. Each has its rules… I have studied the Qur'an. I have evaluated my life through its teachings. I am committed to it, and happy to be so.'

Her views led to confrontation with a number of Islamic religious leaders. From their point of view, she was guilty of insulting conduct because she was ignoring the strict law of the Qur'an that women should keep their bodies covered by the **chador**. For this reason, several Muslim nations do not enter women's teams at international competitions. Episodes like this, eagerly reported in the media, can, in fact, be educational. Many people now better understand some of the problems of having a religious faith. Although media coverage is often biased, nowadays there is a greater effort towards balance and towards an understanding of the clash between religious tradition and modern lifestyles.

THIS POTENT MIXTURE OF GUNS AND GOD

Rabbi calls for suicide bombings

Religious shows to be compulsory on new TV franchises

BURNINGS, BEATINGS, TORTURE.. ANOTHER WEEKEND IN NORTHERN IRELAND

Church failing to attract young as congregations fall by 500,000 in decade

Muslims demand equality in law

 A typical selection of newspaper headlines covering 'religious' issues

Religion in the media

In the past and, to some extent, even today, the media have tended to present **fundamentalist** Islamic views as the 'norm'.

One example of this kind of 'misrepresentation' occurred in the case of Salman Rushdie's book, *The Satanic Verses*. This was described by many Muslims as blasphemous, as an attack on their faith. Fundamentalist Muslims insisted that the author should die, whereas other Muslims have urged followers not to resort to violence. As newspapers at the time pointed out, it is important to remember that, in an Islamic State, Islam *is* the State, and not just the state religion. Rushdie's work was seen by many as an act of treason, punishable by death (**C**).

Public awareness is becoming greater as people become better educated, and it now seems far more acceptable to acknowledge that there are divisions within the same religious traditions, or that certain terrorist groups use religion as an 'excuse' to carry out their activities, or that the media very often focus on negative aspects of a situation in order to boost circulation or to attract audiences.

Two films that have highlighted religious standpoints **D** ▷

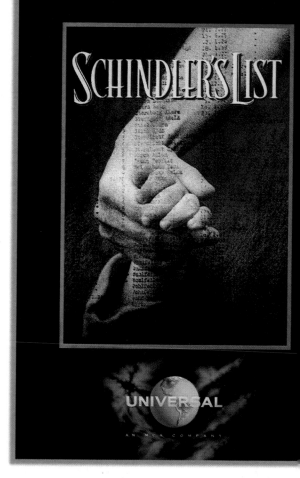

C A balanced report?

A MILLION-DOLLAR bounty was placed on the head of author Salman Rushdie last night as the furore over his novel The Satanic Verses echoed around the world.

The chilling offer was made by one of the Ayatollah Khomeini's aides on Iranian TV, hours after a screaming crowd of 2,000 had stoned the British Embassy in Tehran.

Senior Muslim churchman Hassan Sanei said his June Fifth charity foundation would pay the money – £570,000 – to any foreigner killing the Indian-born writer who lives in Islington, north London.

An Iranian assassin would stand to collect triple bounty – three million dollars – for what Sanei termed 'this holy crusade'.

Rusdie, 41, who was born in Bombay and educated at Cambridge, has reaped the whirlwind since the publication by Viking of The Satanic Verses, which Muslims say is blasphemous and which has already led to riots in which six people died in India and Pakistan. (Only a few weeks ago the author, bearded and sardonic, posed for a photographer from the American Elle magazine to publicise a US tour.

Last night he was clean-shaven, frightened and under armed police guard at a secret hideout. Detectives say he must be protected around the clock for the foreseeable future as Muslim fanatics seek chances to carry out the Ayatollah's execution decree. There are even suggestions that the author may have plastic surgery and emigrate to avoid the Iranian death squads.)

Muslim religious leaders in Britain were yesterday urging their 1.4 million followers not to resort to violence and to observe the law.

But experts believed at least one Iranian hit team may already be on Rushdie's trail. (A sleeper unit of fanatics has probably been activated, according to Ian Geldard, a reseacher at the Institute for the Study of Terrorism.)

He estimated that there were up to 1,000 radical Khomeini supporters in Britain, mainly students or people on short visas. (The main centres were London, Bradford, Leeds and Manchester, particularly among Iranian university students.) 'This is a very serious threat indeed,' added Mr Geldard. 'Khomeini has issued a command – not a suggestion or a hint. A fanatic would obey it to the letter.'

By Anthony Doran, (Daily Mail, 16 February 1989)

In literature today, thousands of titles could be cited to prove that religions play a significant role in the poetry, fiction and drama of even the most non-religious of societies. Many films could also be cited to exemplify the same point. But the world of cinema no longer only produces films based on biblical themes restricted to Christian or Judaic history, as it used to. Nowadays, films tend to examine the world faiths in a more realistic and sympathetic way (**D**).

World religions now make far greater use of the media, instead of the media making use of them. It is not uncommon for religious leaders to be invited to give interviews to the press and television and to be encouraged to speak out about the problems in society. In the United States, religious groups have actually bought television channels, and now broadcast their own programmes to high audience figures.

Finally, we now find God on the internet. Religions are being drawn into making use of the World Wide Web, where ideas of faith, religion and spirituality can be freely examined and discussed. Not everyone approves of this, but there is no doubt that it is important.

On the Web, all the world faiths, as well as tiny religious sects, now have a 'home page'.

Clearly, computer telecommunications are now seen as opportunities to spread religious beliefs and religions are now using a variety of media in a positive way. Some even hope that this global network may bring people together in a way that other forms of the media have failed to do. Television, for example, has tended to take people away from their communities and has encouraged a passive, receptive audience. The internet, it is argued, is creating spiritual communities on a world-wide basis, and placing religious faith firmly in people's lives.

E Religion and the media through the ages

QUESTIONS

1 Read through **C** again, then answer the following questions:

  a What do the words 'bounty' and 'furore' mean? (paragraph 1)

  b What does the term 'reap the whirlwind' mean?

  c Do you think that the article gives a well-balanced account of Muslim attitudes? Give examples from the text in your answer.

2 Select one of the films in **D** and find out what it was about. Comment, in particular, about the theme of the film and the religious concepts and beliefs central to the plot.

3 Either

  a Compare two different newspapers of the same date. Look through them carefully to find any reference to religions or religious topics. For each newspaper, copy and complete a table like the one below to show your findings.

	1	2
Name of newspaper		
Number of religious topics		
Which religion(s)?		
Title of article(s)		
How much detail is given?		
Is the article(s) positive, negative or balanced?		

or b Look at a weekly television or radio magazine. Carefully look through it to find any reference to religions or religious topics. Copy and complete a table like the one below to show your findings.

	Television	Radio
Number of programmes about religions or religious topics		
Which religion(s)?		
Names of religious service programmes		
Names of religious documentary programmes		
Names of religious comedy programmes		

4 'Television always presents religious people as out of touch with the modern world.' Do you agree with this statement? Give reasons for your answer.

ONE WORLD

5

MANY RELIGIONS

Religion and poverty

A

Homelessness is not about individual inadequacy as governments commonly imply. It is caused by the simple fact that there is not enough decent, secure and affordable housing to go round. Shelter believes that everyone, including single people, should have access to decent housing as a basic human right.

Shelter, the National Campaign for Homeless People

stop and think!

- The number of homeless people is increasing each year. Can we rely on charitable organisations such as Shelter (A) to solve this problem?

A home is more than having a roof over one's head. Decent housing certainly means a place that is dry and warm and in reasonable repair. It also means security, privacy, sufficient space, a place where people can grow and make choices. Vandalism, graffiti, fear of violence, lack of play space, all affect how people regard their surroundings.

(Faith in the City: Report of the Archbishop of Canterbury's Commission on Urban Priority Areas)

The homeless

Politicians promise that there will be an end to begging on the streets and their answer to this problem is to implement stricter laws. But many people are forced to beg from others in order to survive. At the moment, these people are breaking the 1824 **Vagrancy** Act under which those who 'place themselves in a public place to beg… are breaking the law'. But a third of all homeless people receive no state benefit, and many have no address to which a benefit could safely be sent. If you have no 'fixed abode' (permanent address) you cannot claim state benefits, and without money you are unlikely to find accommodation. Without either of these you are unlikely to find a job (**A**). Some people are unaware that they are entitled to financial help, and others are too proud to ask for state 'handouts'.

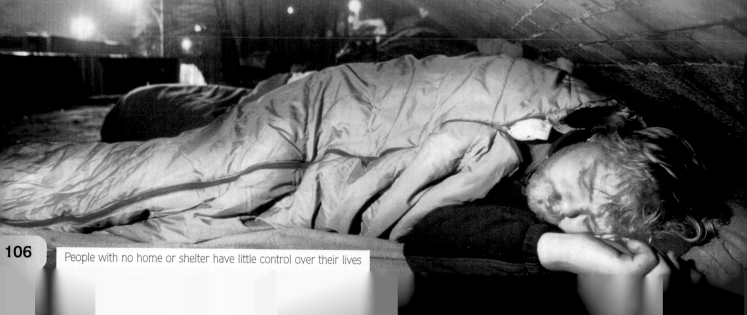

People with no home or shelter have little control over their lives

It is estimated that in 1997 there were about 200,000 young homeless people in Britain. There were approximately 45,000 families in temporary accommodation. About 13,000 families lived in bed and breakfast accommodation.

It is obvious that the wealth of the world is not equally distributed.

Poverty is not confined to overseas countries, but can be seen everywhere. Even in the richest cities, the poor and the homeless are in evidence. Religious leaders throughout the world remind their followers of their duty to help those in need, to relieve poverty. Yet poverty and the homeless remain international problems, and world religions often stand accused either of not being outspoken enough, or of not being actively involved in attempting to resolve the problems.

The religious teachings are clear on the subject of the homeless, and followers are urged to act upon them (**B**, **C** and **D**).

B Christian teaching

Selling their possessions and goods, they gave to anyone as he had need.
Acts 2:45

But when you give a banquet, invite the poor, the crippled, the lame, the blind, and you will be blessed. Although they cannot repay you, you will be repaid at the resurrection ...
Luke 14:13–14

C Muslim teaching

Alms are for the poor and needy, and those employed to administer the (funds).
Qur'an surah 9:60

But do good; for Allah loves those who do good.
Qur'an surah 2:195

D Sikh teaching

When a man is weak with the pangs of poverty and hunger, has no money and no one to offer him consolation, when he has no one to help him in his need and all his work comes to nothing, let him remember the Supreme Lord and he will have an everlasting kingdom.
Adi Granth 70

Only he who earns a living by the sweat of his brow and shares his earnings with others has discovered the path of righteousness.
Adi Granth 1245

QUESTIONS

1 What is your definition of 'homelessness'?

2 What do you think are the three main causes of homelessness?

3 What are your thoughts on the Church of England's definition of homelessness?

4 It is considered that some people (because of their age, income or race) are more likely to become homeless than others. Which people do you think are more likely to be homeless? Give reasons for your answer.

5 Whose responsibility are the homeless? Give reasons for your answer.

6 How might the homeless escape the trap they are in?

7 What do the teachings of Christianity and Islam expect followers to do for those less well off than themselves?

8 In your opinion, should religious followers be doing something for those less well off than themselves? Explain why.

Poverty: fac

Why do rich and poor people exist within society? Why are there some 'rich' (developed) countries yet so many 'poor' (developing) countries? It is not beyond the capacity of the richer nations to give assistance to reduce the incidence of poverty and hardship to much smaller proportions. Unfortunately, the necessary decisions have not been taken either by individuals or governments.

People often have widely differing views about why there are different levels of wealth throughout the world. Some of these ideas are set out below in **A** to **I**.

stop and think!

- What do you understand by the following terms: poor country; rich country; poverty; multinational company; raw materials?

- How many ways can you think of to complete these four sentences?

  A person becomes poor because...

  A person becomes wealthy because...

  Some countries become poor because...

  Some countries become wealthy because...

A There has always been poverty, and there always will be. If people want to live in slums and have more children than they can feed, then that's their business.

B Sooner or later, the poorer countries will get together and force the richer countries to give them a fairer deal.

C There are too many people to feed and clothe. There must be better birth control in poorer countries.

D Poorer countries do not want emergency supplies of food when it's too late. They want the seeds to plant, so that they can feed themselves.

E The increase in unemployment in many of the poorer countries is due to the expertise and technology of the richer countries. Advice and loans help to buy imported machines which mean that local people lose jobs, and governments pay high interest rates.

or fiction?

Muslim Aid

Muslim Aid began work from a small office in London, in November 1985. The charity was set up by 23 leading Muslim organisations in response to a series of disasters in Ethiopia, Afghanistan, Bangladesh and Palestine.

Its aim was to alleviate poverty and provide relief for the victims of wars and natural disasters. By 1989, its operations had expanded and millions of pounds of emergency aid had been distributed throughout Africa, Asia and Europe.

As Muslim Aid grew, the nature of its work began to change. Whilst continuing its commitment to emergency relief work, Muslim Aid started to implement long-term development programmes. This was achieved through education and skills training, credit and agricultural schemes, water and healthcare projects.

Healthcare programmes range from one-day child immunisation camps in Bangladesh, to full-scale healthcare programmes, such as in Somalia, which employs 200 doctors and nursing staff to provide basic medical treatment to a target population of 500,000 people.

> He is not a believer who eats his fill while his neighbour remains hungry by his side.
> *Hadith*

> The poor countries are poor because of their climate and local environment – the tropical heat, the poor soils, the dense jungles, the deserts, the mosquitoes and the lack of clean water.

> Giving poorer countries modern technology is not the answer. They do not need tractors which they can't afford to maintain; they need more efficient ways of using the tools they already have.

> If we identify those multi national companies responsible for buying raw materials too cheaply from poorer countries, we could put pressure on them by not buying their goods.

> The hundreds of millions who are dying of malnourishment are the responsibility of the richer nations who persuaded poorer countries to stop growing their own food, and to grow flowers, for example, for export.

Education and skills training

Thousands of people have been helped through training and sharing of skills. Interest-free loans have enabled them to work and to be able to take care of themselves and their families.

Clean water and sanitation

Muslim Aid provides the resources and skills to install hand pumps, deep-tube and brick-lined wells for communities in rural areas of Asia and Africa.

Muslim Aid in Britain

One of the many groups to benefit from help has been the Muslim Women's Helpline. This was launched in 1989 to offer practical support and advice to women throughout Britain. Support is also given to counselling services, education programmes and youth services.

QUESTIONS

1 Read the statements A to I and decide if each statement is fact or opinion. Copy and complete a table like the one below to explain your answers.

Statement	Fact	Opinion
A		
B		
C		
D		
E		
F		
G		
H		
I		

2 Find out about the work of Christian Aid or CAFOD (see page 79) and compare their work with the work of Muslim Aid.

1 Why do you think the Western way of life and Buddhism do not mix well together?

2 In Romans 13:13 it states 'Let us behave decently.' What do you think the writer means by 'behaving decently'?

3 Give three reasons why a place of worship is regarded as the centre of a faith community.

4 What are the two main reasons given for the use of artwork in the Christian tradition?

5 Why is calligraphy such an important feature of Islamic faith?

6 Why are there no pictures, statues or photographs of human beings in a mosque?

7 'The media normally portrays religions in a negative way.' Do you agree or disagree with this statement? Give examples to support your viewpoint.

8 One headline (page 103) states that the Church is failing to attract young people. Do you think this is true? Give reasons to explain your answer.

9 What is a hymn?

10 What particular problems does a female athlete face if she comes from a Muslim background?

11 Why do you think fundamentalist views are so often portrayed in the media?

12 Why do you think the internet is being increasingly used by religious groups?

13 Describe and explain the range of religious programmes provided by either the BBC or ITV.

14 **a** Describe, analyse and explain the way in which a religious issue has been dealt with in either a TV drama, a film or a soap opera.

b Choose one of these programmes and evaluate the reasons why it might be popular with some viewers, but unpopular with others.

15 Give your own response to 'You don't need to go to a church to be a good Christian.' Give reasons for your answer.

16 According to the extract from 'Faith in the City', page 106, what is a 'home'?

17
a When you think of a homeless person, what sort of person do you imagine?
b The following things are sometimes described as signs of poverty in Britain. Select four of these and explain how they can affect the quality of a person's life.
- relying on social security
- poor health
- living in a high crime-rate area
- unemployment
- not having a car
- poor housing
- little educational success
- domestic problems

18 Describe and explain how Christian or Muslim teachings could help to relieve the problem of homelessness.

19 Describe the work of one agency working for the poor.

20 Explain, using the religious viewpoints you have studied, any advice given about the responsibilities of the wealthy towards the poor.

21 In a world where many people are starving and homeless, religious people cannot be true to their faith and remain rich.' Do you agree with this statement? Give your views showing that you have considered different points of view.

22 Explain in your own words what is meant by poverty and wealth.

23 Describe what Muslim Aid is and what functions it performs.

24 Why do you think education is such an important part of Muslim Aid's work? What sort of education is necessary?

25 Why have groups such as Muslim Aid or Christian Aid been reluctant to give just money to help the poor in the developing world?

Introduction
One world

Unit aims

The aims of this unit are to introduce you to some of the greatest problems facing the human race today. As the range of religious viewpoints is closely examined, you will find that even within the same religious tradition there is close agreement in some issues, but that in other areas, there are important differences.

Key concepts

Within any one particular religious faith there has never been a unanimous agreement about violence and punishment in society. Most people condemn those who use violence, but it is generally accepted that when there is a war, members of the armed forces may kill. We also have to accept that punishing people hurts them and can be regarded as cruel. As we explore these issues, we shall see how the religious teachings relate to them.

What is this unit about?

We can see from history that some of the most fanatical wars have been brought about by religion. This unit examines the attitudes to war that we find in the teachings and writings of the world religions. All of them recognise their responsibility for promoting peace, for reconciliation and forgiveness. And yet, in practice, it is clear that religious people remain as divided as everyone else about war.

In today's world, there are clear indications that millions of people are deprived of the human rights and fair treatment that most of us tend to take for granted. Religious leaders are increasingly concerned with injustice, prejudice, discrimination and the pursuit of human rights. All the religions agree that the rules of justice have to be applied in the same way to all similar cases.

Every religion provides guidelines as to how people should behave. Many of these rules are demanding and not easy to follow. Every society has based its 'laws' on such guidelines but inevitably there will be 'law breakers' and we need to be protected from such individuals.

many problems

The question which arises is how to enforce the set laws justly and deal with people who break them. All the teachings are agreed that no one should be above the law or beneath the protection of the law. The ultimate punishment is clearly the death penalty and, within this unit, the arguments 'for' and 'against' are clearly set out. Although the vast majority of religious faiths firmly oppose the taking of life, certain religions permit the use of execution. To understand this apparent contradiction we have to examine their teachings very closely and bear in mind that, in certain countries, the religion *is* the state, not the state religion. In other words, state and religion are tied together and if execution is the policy held by the government of a country, then the religious leaders are not in a position to oppose it.

War and

Central to the teachings of all the world religions is the concept of peace, and yet throughout history, religious people have been divided over whether it is right to use violence or be involved in war or armed conflict.

Every day, newspaper headlines and television heat up this debate with reports of conflicts, and gruesome or sensational events. This makes for large audience figures and increases the circulation figures, so editors find themselves pressurised into continuing to satisfy this morbid fascination.

The word 'conflict' is often used to denote violent physical acts, but it also can be used in many situations, such as disputes, competition and conflict of interests. Wars occur when the level of conflict reaches a national, international or global sphere (**A**).

Christianity

Initially, Christians were pacifists, opposing any form of resistance – to the extent of not even defending themselves when they were being persecuted and facing death in the Roman arenas. Yet, after the conversion of the Emperor Constantine to Christianity, it became acceptable for Christians to be in the army, and, some time later, all serving soldiers were expected to be Christians! Today, there is still much debate over the issue of war, and opinions remain divided even among followers of the same religion (**B**).

Islam

A misleading image of Muslims engaged in conflict is frequently promoted in the western media. To assume that the Muslim religion is typified by the activities of extreme fundamentalist groups would be as unfair as stating that the IRA represents Christian groups. All Muslims believe that it is their duty to defend themselves against any threat to Islam.

The word jihad, so frequently associated with war, is misapplied and misused in the West. Contrary to popular belief, it does not mean 'holy war'. It means 'to strive or struggle in the name of Allah'. In the warfare sense, jihad is permitted in self defence, to protect an individual's life, family and home, and also to fight oppression (**C**).

A The different levels of conflict

- Personal
- Two people
- Within or between small groups
- Within or between large groups or the individual, or small groups against large groups
- National (within one state)
- International (involving two or more states)
- Worldwide/global (affecting everyone)

B Christian teaching

Make plans by seeking advice; if you wage war, obtain guidance.
Proverbs 20:18

A time to kill and a time to heal, a time to tear down and a time to build . . . a time to love and a time to hate, a time for war and a time for peace.
Ecclesiastes 3:3,8

. . . Nation will not take up sword against nation, nor will they train for war any more.
Micah 4:3

There is deceit in the hearts of those who plot evil, but joy for those who promote peace.
Proverbs 12:20

 C Muslim teaching

To those against whom war is made, permission is given (to fight), because they are wronged.
Qur'an surah 22:39

peace

Buddhism

A Buddhist must have compassion for any living creature, even to the extent of not killing an insect! It is clear, therefore that any aspect of war is unacceptable (**D**).

All (wars) stem from our lack of human understanding, of mutual trust, and of mutual respect, based on kindness and love for all beings.

The Dalai Lama

D Buddhist teaching

What is the enduring meaning of Buddhism? Basically, I think, it is compassion, not limited to human kind, but extended to all the living creatures. I think that is the essence, the compassion. Without that, I think there is nothing else.

Worlds of Faith, *by John Bowker, Ariel Books, 1983*

stop and think!

How do the Buddhist teachings support Christian beliefs in pacifism?

PEACE!

QUESTIONS

Use **A** to describe the level of conflict in each of the examples in the list below.

1 Homelessness

2 Football hooligans

3 Environmental pollution

4 Suicide

5 Murder

Religions and

It is rare when there is a single, clear cause for the outbreak of war. Wars have been fought out of fear, protest against injustice, and because of the actions of evil individuals or corrupt governments.

Some of the most fanatical struggles have been inspired and legitimised by religion. The results i each case are the same: loss of life, destruction, mental and physical suffering, enormous debts and a huge refugee problem.

The Crusades

Christian soldiers involved in the Crusade campaigns in the 11th to 13th centuries felt they were fighting on behalf of God against the **infidels** or **pagans** who were living in the Holy Land and occupying the holy city of Jerusalem. It was Pope Urban II himself who urged the Crusaders to 'rescue the Holy Land from that dreadful race'. He added: 'All men going there who die, whether on the journey or while fighting the pagans will immediately be forgiven their sins.' This was a ver powerful incentive for some men to join the crusading armies (**A**).

Emperor Frederick II of Germany leads the Sixth Crusade into Jerusalem in 1229 **A**

eachings on war

Islam

he concept of 'holy war' does not exist in Islamic teachings, but there
s 'just war' which allows for the establishment of justice, self defence
ind protection of one's family. Oppression has no place in Islamic
eachings and, on occasions, in order to overthrow it, war has been seen
is a necessary evil (**B**).

Christianity

t has been argued by Christian denominations, such as the Society of
Friends (Quakers) and the Anabaptists, that the only true position a
Christian can adopt is one of absolute pacifism. Teachings such as **C**
einforce their views.

Sikhism

he first Sikh community founded by Guru Nanak followed a simple
disciplined way of life, committed to strict pacifism. As Sikh fortunes
luctuated, later Gurus taught their followers that they should be
prepared to defend themselves. The 'kirpan', originally a sword used by
Sikhs to defend themselves, has become a symbol of dignity and self
espect, and a reminder of the need to protect the individual's religious
reedom.

stop and think!

- What do B and D tell us about the Muslim and Sikh views of war and peace?

B Muslim teaching

Fight in the cause of Allah those who fight you, but do not transgress limits... if they cease, let there be no hostility except to those who practise oppression.

Qur'an surah 2:190,193

C Christian teaching

You have heard that it was said, 'Eye for eye, and tooth for tooth.' But I tell you, Do not resist an evil person. If someone strikes you on the right cheek, turn to him the other also.

Matthew 5:38–39

... for all who draw the sword will die by the sword.

Matthew 26:52

D Sikh teaching

The Khalsa – pure ones – shall rule, no hostile powers shall exist... Those who enter the Khalsa for shelter will be protected. Without power, justice does not flourish, without justice everything is crushed and ruined.

Dasam Granth

QUESTIONS

'Positive and effective non-violence is the alternative we offer to warfare.' (Quaker Peace Testimony For Today)

1 What price are we prepared to pay for peace?

2 Are there any circumstances when it is morally right for Christians to take part in a war?

A Muhammad Ali when he was World Champion

Opinions on war and peace

From the outside, it often appears that followers of Christianity or Islam do not hold a consistent or coherent attitude when considering the topic of war. Every individual is unique and similarly, each person's responses to a particular situation will vary.

Teachings in these two religions are consistent but can be interpreted in differing ways. Some choose to adopt the stance of individuals such as Dr Martin Luther King, the black Civil Rights leader in the USA (1929–68), and 'Mahatma' Gandhi, the Indian leader (1869–1948). Others clearly believe that war can be justified in self defence to fight oppression, or to put right injustice.

We clearly see the different viewpoints when we examine the stand taken by two individuals: Muhammad Ali (**A**) and Leonard Cheshire (**D**).

118

B The escalation and brutal nature of the conflict in Vietnam

Muhammad Ali

Muhammad Ali (formerly known as Cassius Clay) became the World Heavyweight Boxing Champion in 1964. He converted from Christianity to Islam, and was totally opposed to the fighting going on between the USA and North Vietnam. He soon found himself at the heart of a nation in upheaval, and became a spokesperson against the politics of war, religion and race that were tearing America apart in the 1960s.

One act of defiance was to cost Ali his Heavyweight Crown and three and a half of his best years banned from the ring. In 1966, as the US Army's need for manpower grew, Ali was called up in the draft of young men aged 18 to 24 years. He refused, and by doing so, gave up everything he had won and earned – his boxing titles, his career and his fortune. He had been one of America's favourite heroes, but now he became one of the most hated.

On 28 April 1967, he turned down his final chance, stating at a press conference: 'No. I will not go 10,000 miles from here to help murder and kill another poor people simply to continue the domination of white slave masters over the darker people of the earth.'

The US Court had no sympathy for his religious scruples and he received a maximum ten thousand dollar fine and five years imprisonment (later suspended on appeal). Ali's response was typically defiant: 'Clean up my cell and take me to jail!'

Overnight, he became a civil rights **martyr.** Reactions to him were mixed. According to some, Ali had 'given up being a man' when he did not support the war effort. Others felt that he had every right to be a **conscientious objector**. Muhammad Ali lived for fame but threw it all away when it was against his religious principles. His courage in the boxing ring was never questioned, but like so many other conscientious objectors, he was regarded by some as cowardly and unpatriotic.

Opinions on war and peace

C The scene that Leonard Cheshire witnessed as the second atomic bomb exploded over Nagasaki

Leonard Cheshire

Leonard Cheshire was Britain's official observer when the second atomic bomb was dropped on Nagasaki, in Japan. Cheshire was one of the RAF's youngest and most decorated Group Captains, and had established himself as one of the greatest bomber pilots of the Second World War. He was awarded the Victoria Cross for four years of 'sustained heroism', flying over 100 bombing missions, which inevitably caused deaths.

Yet the same man, years later, was described in a newspaper article as 'closer to sainthood than any other person in Britain this century'. So, how did this transformation come about?

What he witnessed on the 9 August 1945 shocked him. Over Nagasaki, he saw a huge ball of fire rushing upwards, leaving behind it a mushroom-shaped cloud. This is a transcript of his description of the event:

'There was this really awesome sight… you could not think of the city, you could think of nothing. Your eyes were riveted by this fireball rocketing upwards. The fire died out and became a kind of yellow sulphurous cloud and it was suspended on a column and my impression was that the column was symmetrical not jagged like high explosive. It was almost finely sculptured and it was rising at an enormous speed but effortlessly and there was something all the more frightening in it because it was so effortless… bubbling like a cauldron… suddenly your thoughts would stop and cut and you would think about the people underneath.'

After the Second World War, Cheshire became a Roman Catholic, and dedicated his life to helping disabled people, setting up Cheshire Homes throughout the world. With very little money, he set out to find support for his idea of nursing homes for disabled people. He discovered a new role for himself, and in so doing, brought new life to many who would otherwise have suffered in their final years.

D Leonard Cheshire

Unlike Muhammad Ali, Cheshire had made a large contribution to the war effort, and he was able to reconcile this with his religious beliefs. Ali, on the other hand, intent on hurting his opponent and knocking him out in a boxing ring, was sure that fighting in a war was against his religious beliefs.

It is easy to feel confused by quotes from various religious scriptures that are sometimes misused to justify or denounce war. It often appears that followers of the world religions do not have a consistent or coherent attitude when considering war. This is clearly seen in **E** below.

stop and think!

- Looking at E, can you explain why there is no clear agreed view of 'just war' among religious people?

E

If a person intends to kill you, be the first to kill him.
The Talmud

Turn from evil and do good; seek peace and pursue it.
Psalm 34:14

Teachings can always be interpreted in different ways. Some individuals known as conscientious objectors cross all the religious barriers in their opposition to wars, holding a view similar to that held by Buddhists.

In the past, people who refused to fight in a war because of their principles often faced criticism and abuse. Some individuals during the First World War were imprisoned, and many received a white feather which represented cowardice. In the United States, the people who protested against the Vietnam War and refused to fight are still regarded with suspicion today. Young men who ignored the draft, like Muhammad Ali, were described as unpatriotic, and some were severely punished for their beliefs.

F Would you be willing to go to prison for your beliefs?

QUESTIONS

1 Nuclear bombs and other weapons which maim and kill indiscriminately oppose the concepts of all world religions because it is inevitable that innocent people will suffer. Non-combatants must be spared and the environment must be protected. Does the threat of nuclear war make any difference when assessing the conditions set out for a just war?

2 It has been argued that the atomic bombs brought the Second World War to a quick end thereby avoiding further bloodshed. In view of this, do you think the bombings of

Hiroshima and Nagasaki were morally justified? Give your reasons.

3 Many Christians fought in the Second World War against Nazi Germany. On what grounds might they argue that their actions were morally justifiable?

4 How would you feel if you were called up to fight in a war?

5 Do you think conscientious objectors could be described as cowards?

6 In what circumstances, if any, would you be prepared to die for your beliefs?

121

A just war?

Throughout history, millions of lives have been affected by warfare. Some people, as we have seen, do not believe that it is right to fight under any circumstances. Others are content to judge the 'morality' of each war by a set of rules – the conditions of war.

Conditions for a just war

The two original conditions for a just war (**B**) were set out by St Augustine and a third condition (**D**) was added by St Thomas Aquinas. A fourth condition was added in the 16th century by Francisco de Vittoria. For several centuries these conditions seemed satisfactory, but by the 19th century, three additional conditions were needed (**E**). It is important to remember that in the modern world, nations possess weapons capable of total devastation, weaponry which was not foreseen by St Augustine and St Aquinas.

A St Augustine (AD 354 to 430) was a writer of great importance. His ideas shaped the development of Christianity and his thought dominated the Middle Ages.

B The two original conditions for a just war

> 1 There is a just cause. In practice, this can only happen when a country is attacked and has to defend itself. Armed conflict is only justified if an aggressor refuses to restore what has been seized.
>
> 2 The war can only be declared and controlled by the ruler or governing body of the country concerned [i.e. it cannot be waged by private citizens].
>
> *St Augustine*

C St Thomas Aquinas (AD c.1225 to 1274) became the official theologian of the Roman Catholic Church. He is credited with interpreting St Augustine's original thinking, formulating the Just War criteria.

D A further condition for a just war

> 3 The war has a clear and just aim and all fighting must stop once that aim has been achieved. It also means that the ultimate goal must be to restore good relations with the enemy, not to humiliate him.
>
> *St Thomas Aquinas*

stop and think!

• **Do you think that the conditions set out by St Augustine and St Aquinas would be helpful to nations today faced with the possibility of war?**

E Four further conditions for a just war

4 It is waged in a just way. In other words, limits must be put in place: first by restricting the amount of force to the maximum needed for the objectives to be achieved: second, by ensuring the safety of all non-combatants and all those not directly involved in the war effort.

Francisco de Vittoria

5 There is a reasonable chance of success. Obviously it would be wrong to lose thousands of lives, knowing that there was no chance of winning.

6 Every other possibility of solving the conflict has been tried before the war is declared – this must include detailed and wide-ranging negotiations at every stage. War can only be declared as a last resort.

7 The good achieved as a result of the war must outweigh the evil which led to the war. Even suffering on a mass scale might be a lesser evil than allowing an aggressor to continue a murderous regime.

F Hindu teaching

If you do not fight in this just war, you will neglect your duty, harm your reputation and commit the sin of omission. Having regard to your duty, you should not hesitate, because for a warrior there is nothing greater than a just war.

Bhagavad Gita 2:31,33

G Muslim teaching

To those against whom war is made, permission is given (to fight), because they are wronged – and verily, Allah is most powerful for their aid.

Qur'an surah 22:39

imilar themes of the just war can be seen in the teachings of other world religions such as Hinduism (**F**) and Islam (**G**). Both religions set out lear conditions for when military action is justified.

The Gulf War

/ar in the Arabian Gulf prompted a debate within the Christian Church about whether it /as a 'just' conflict. The Pope condemned the terrible logic of war' and declared the Gulf War injust. Other Church leaders disagreed, believing that the war was justified because a people had to be liberated. In the Arab world, houghts were divided and Muslims were set against Muslims.

Distinguishing between political, economic and eligious ideas is not easy, and it would be fair to say that very few wars, from the Crusades to modern-day conflicts, could honestly be described as 'Holy Wars' or 'Just Wars'.

QUESTIONS

1 Choose any war to research, and using the seven conditions in **B**, **D** and **E**, decide whether or not this war can be described as 'just'. For each condition, explain how it was or was not satisfied.

2

I want to know who the men in the shadows are

I want to hear somebody ask them why

They can be counted on to tell us who our enemies are

But they're never the ones to fight or to die.

From the song 'Lives In the Balance' by Jackson Browne

a What do you think Jackson Browne is saying in his song above?

b Who are the 'men in the shadows'?

Letters from

These extracts are from letters sent home by young soldiers fighting in Vietnam.

A

This country is so beautiful when the sun's shining on the mountains. The farmers in their paddy fields with their water buffalo and palm trees, monkeys, birds and even the strange insects... For a fleeting moment I am not in a war zone at all, just on vacation but still missing you and the family.

A soldier fighting in Vietnam

B

Dear Mum and Dad
You know that joke about how hard it is to tell the good guys from the bad guys? Well, it's funny in the Bronx but not over here. The enemy in our area of operations is a farmer by day and VC [Vietcong] by night ...

D An anxious Vietnamese family are evacuated from their village

C US soldiers brutally torturing a Vietcong prisoner

E

Dear Mum
The days are fairly peaceful but the nights are pure hell. I look up at the stars. It's so hard to believe the same stars shine over you in such a different world.
All my love
Al

F

Dear Mum
Anyone over here who walks more than fifty feet through elephant grass should automatically get a Purple Heart [highest bravery award]. Try to imagine grass possessing razor sharp edges, 8 to 15 feet high, so thick as to cut visibility to one yard. Then try to imagine walking through it while all around you are men possessing the latest automatic weapons who desperately want to kill you. You would be amazed how much a man can age in one patrol.

Vietnam

H With all the death and destruction I've seen in the past week, I've aged greatly. I feel like an old man now. I've seen enough of war and its destruction. I'm scared by it but not scared enough to quit... Please pray for us all here at Khe Sanh.
Your son, Kevin

G We are all scared. One can easily see this emotion in the eyes of each individual. One might hide it with his mouth, while another might hide it with his actions but there is no way round it... we are all scared.

J Well, you learn everyday the mistakes you are making but the biggest one is to get too attached to any one person. Not over here at least! Things happen so quickly and one minute he's fine, the next he's not. But old Don is pretty lucky – knock on wood! Home I'll come I'm sure.
Love Don
(Days later, 2nd Lt Donald Jacques, along with 22 of his men, was killed in an ambush just outside Khe Sanh.)

I US troops in Vietnam

stop and think!
• How do all the accounts in these letters contrast with the images of war seen in films?

QUESTIONS

1 What do you think is the main difference between **A** and **F**?

2 In **F**, **G** and **H**, what images of war are the writers portraying?

3 The following is an extract from *The Tarnished Shield* by George Walton (Dodd, 1973). This is a true account of the My Lai massacre by American troops led by Lt William Calley:

'Within My Lai Four, the killings had become more sadistic. Several old men were stabbed with bayonets and one was thrown down a well to be followed by a hand grenade. Some women and children praying outside... were killed by shooting them in the back of the head with rifles. Occasionally a soldier would drag a girl, often a mere child to a ditch where he would rape her... the young were slaughtered with the same impartiality as the old.'

4 **a** Do you agree with the statement 'in war, anything goes'?

b Is it possible to win a war in a humane and honourable way?

Prejudice and

A Prejudice can take many forms

Nationality

Gender

Disabilities

Colour

PREJUDICE AND DISCRIMINATION

Age

Social Class

Wealth

Beliefs

stop and think!

- What, in your opinion, is the most common type of prejudice? Give some examples to support your case.

B Buddhist teaching

May all beings have happiness, and the causes of happiness; may all be free from sorrow and the causes of sorrow, may all never be separated from the sacred happiness which is sorrowless. And may all live in equanimity [calmness], without too much attachment and too much aversion [hatred], and live believing in the equality of all that lives.

Tibetan Buddhist prayer

C Muslim teaching

And among His signs is the creation of the heavens and the earth and the variations in your languages and your colours; verily in that are Signs for those who know.

Qur'an surah 30:22

World religions have attracted believers from many different countries and races, and it would seem that religion should act as a unifying factor. Most religious followers will claim that everyone is equal. Belief, however, is one thing and practice is another.

Attitudes of prejudice and discrimination affect our everyday lives. Prejudice means pre-judging a person or a group on inadequate information. Discrimination is best described as 'prejudice in action' – when, because of prejudice, an individual or group is unfairly treated. Such unfair treatment can take many forms in our society (**A**).

Religion often stands accused of creating divisions rather than breaking down barriers. Many believe that people of different faiths must show the way, sharing their views, learning from one another. Buddhism, for example, recognises that people grow up ignorant of others and of their ways. It is essential to realise that people of all colours, race, gender and age, are subject to the same problems of suffering. Shantideva, an Indian Buddhist Master once stated: 'Whatever joy there is in the world, all comes from desiring others to be happy, and whatever suffering there is in this world all comes from desiring myself to be happy.'

True wisdom reverses the ignorance and selfishness which contribute to prejudice and discrimination. Buddhists reject the idea that there are differences between people and things. They are concerned that people may hold extremist views, often based on lack of knowledge and understanding (**B**).

The Muslim faith views prejudice and discrimination, whether open or hidden, as evil. The teachings found in the Qur'an are clear: that people of different colour, race or traditions are not to be unjustly treated (**C**).

D In the notorious Nazi death camp, Auschwitz, prisoners stand at the electrified fence which separates them from the outside world

discrimination

The position of all Muslims in relation to other religious faiths is one of tolerance to the extent that it is a sacred duty to protect the freedom of belief for other religious followers. In Islam, colour, class, and wealth should make no difference in the sight of Allah.

At some time or another all the religious faiths have been subjected to prejudice and discrimination. The most notable example is that of Judaism which, throughout the centuries, has been subjected to repeated persecution.

The treatment of Jews at the hands of the Nazis during the Second World War was horrific, and clearly reveals what happens when prejudice and discrimination are encouraged. Millions of Jews were murdered, along with countless numbers of mentally handicapped people, gypsies and homosexuals. This terrible period in the history of humanity is called the Holocaust (**D**).

It is noticeable that religious faiths, too, have been guilty of prejudice and should not be excluded from criticism. There have been numerous episodes of fighting between groups of the same religious tradition, such as Roman Catholics opposing Protestants in Northern Ireland; Christians and Muslims in Beirut; and Sikhs fighting Hindus. True, these often represent the actions of fanatics, but such images often give very negative and mixed messages. One religious tradition often singled out for encouraging prejudice is Hinduism. It is important to stress that Hinduism teaches people to respect and love others, but nevertheless Indian society stands accused today of the caste system which still exists; although it has long been banned. The varna system, as it is known, still exerts a powerful influence and creates division not just amongst Hindus but also amongst Sikhs and Buddhists (**E**).

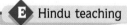

E Hindu teaching

When the Primal Man was divided the Brahmin [priest] arose from his mouth, the Kshatriya [soldier] from his arms, the Vaishya [merchant] from his thighs and the Shudra [worker] from his feet.

Rig Veda, Purusha Hymn

F What is your reaction to this photo?

QUESTIONS

1 Why do you think religious people are so often victims of prejudice and discrimination? Try to give several reasons in your answer – the photos in **D** and **F** should provide you with some clues.

2 The world religions teach people to respect others and yet we still see discrimination. Why do you think this is?

Crime and punishment

An individual can break a moral law by lying or a religious law by misusing God's name. This behaviour does not constitute a crime unless the state has made a law which forbids such actions. According to the Oxford Dictionary a crime is 'an offence punishable by law'. In order to ensure the smooth running of a society, there has to be some kind of legal system based on laws, law enforcers and punishment. This sounds straightforward enough, but not everyone agrees with the ways in which crime is interpreted and recorded. More importantly, there is a great deal of controversy concerning the punishments handed out to offenders.

A A letter from Lucien Lawrence, Philip Lawrence's son, highlights the pain and grief caused to a victim's family

Dear Father christmas,
I hope you are well and not to cold.
I hope you wont think that I am being a nuisance but I have changed my mind what I want for christmas. I wanted to have a telescope but now I want to have my daddy back because without my to help to daddy to help I will not able to see the stars anyway.
I am the only boy in the family now but I am not very big and I need my daddy to help me to stop my mummy and sisters from crying.
Love from
Lucien Lawrence
age 8

shine

The death of Philip Lawrence, a headmaster murdered just outside his school in 1996 trying to stop one of his students from being attacked, provoked a public outcry concerning what is perceived as the 'state of youth today'.

All the world religions agree that an offender must not be allowed to get away with a crime, but all too often they disagree over the aims of punishment.

The teachings of some religions imply that the punishment should match the crime as closely as possible. Both Muslim and Jewish teachings seem to suggest that revenge is an important aim of punishment, but this can be misleading. The Muslim teaching in **B** emphasises the need for forgiveness and the often quoted Jewish teaching in **C** was designed as a restraint from excessive revenge and punishment.

B Muslim teaching

The recompense [reward] for an injury is an injury equal thereto; but if a person forgives and makes reconciliation, his reward is due from Allah.

Qur'an surah 42:40

C Jewish teaching

If anyone take the life of a human being, he must be put to death. If anyone injures his neighbour, whatever he has done must be done to him: fracture for fracture, eye for eye, tooth for tooth. As he has injured the other, so he is to be injured.

Leviticus 24:17,19–20

D Inmates from Strangeways prison riot because of the poor conditions in prison and alleged brutal treatment

It is important not to misinterpret such sayings. It would be wrong to imply that Islamic or Jewish laws on crime and punishment are unduly harsh. In these societies, these laws are to ensure that not only is justice done, but also that it is seen to be done.

While accepting that any crime which **destabilises** society is viewed seriously, most of the world religions appear to question whether it is ever right to hurt others, no matter what they have done. Buddhists, in particular, try to steer a path between punishment and forgiveness (**E**).

stop and think!

• Is the Buddhist viewpoint realistic in this day and age?

QUESTIONS

1 What do such headlines tell us about the way in which the media reports crimes?

LIFE FOR THE 'VULTURES' WHO MURDERED

TOWN OF TERROR

2 When passing sentence on an offender, should the court take into account any of the following:

a previous record?
b state of health?
c home background?

d age and gender?
e psychiatric report?

129

Society faces a problem with some of its members who do not want to adhere to the rules. The aims of punishment are to find a way to deal with criminals and at the same time, protect society and the individual.

Studies suggest that harsh punishments do not always get the best results. Offenders build up resentment towards the 'system', and, when released, try to seek revenge on society. This situation can easily spiral to become a vicious circle (**B**).

Traditionally, punishment has six purposes, and most sentences handed out to offenders are a mixture of several of these.

The aims of

Punishment

1 Deterrence
It is hoped that the punishment will discourage the person from repeating the crime. It is also hoped that the fear of a punishment will stop other individuals from committing crimes.

2 Protection
Punishment by locking someone up is a way of protecting society from the anti-social behaviour of some people. Some types of punishment also attempt to protect the offender as well as society.

3 Retribution
Based on the idea of an eye for an eye. If someone has done something wrong they should be given a punishment that fits the crime.

4 Reform
Punishment should not only stop people from continuing to commit crimes, but should help them to become responsible members of society.

5 Reparation
If someone breaks the law, they must be prepared to make amends, in other words, pay back something to the victim or to society.

6 Vindication
For people to live together and to feel safe the law must be respected and be seen to be upheld.

A The scales of justice: are they always fair?

stop
and
think!

- What is meant by the term 'vicious circle'?

- When punishing offenders how can we try to minimise their resentment?

It is possible to find elements of these six aims of punishments in most religious teachings. The emphasis is nearly always on protection and reforming the criminal but in western society the remaining aims are often regarded as equally, if not more, important.

stop and think!

- Look at the Christian teachings in C and then try to match them up to the six aims of punishment set out on the opposite page.

B Harsh punishment can lead to a vicious circle

1 minor offence

2 harsh punishment

4 major offence

3 revenge

punishment

 C Christian teaching

> Rescue me, O Lord, from evil men; protect me from men of violence. Keep me, O Lord, from the hands of the wicked; protect me from men of violence who plan to trip my feet.
>
> *Psalm 140:1,4*

> Do not withhold discipline from a child; if you punish him with the rod, he will not die. Punish him with the rod and save his soul from death.
>
> *Proverbs 23:13*

> If a man steals an ox or a sheep and slaughters it or sells it, he must pay back five head of cattle for the ox and four sheep for the sheep.
>
> *Exodus 22:1*

> Then all the men of his town shall stone him to death. You must purge the evil from among you. All Israel will hear of it and be afraid.
>
> *Deuteronomy 21:21*

> But if there is serious injury, you are to take life for life, eye for eye, tooth for tooth, hand for hand, foot for foot, burn for burn, wound for wound, bruise for bruise.
>
> *Exodus 21:23–5*

> Consequently, he who rebels against the authority is rebelling against what God has instituted, and those who do so will bring judgement on themselves.
>
> *Romans 13:2*

The aims of punishment

All the world religions accept the need to protect individuals from criminals, and urge their followers to lead a law-abiding life and not to associate with wrongdoers (**D**).

Imprisonment, as a punishment for criminal acts, only developed in the nineteenth century. Until this time, people were temporarily placed in prisons while awaiting punishment. The three main types of punishment were execution, **banishment** or fines. During the nineteenth century, a large number of prisons were built and some are still in use today. Many copied the Pentonville prison design, like the spokes of a wheel – long corridors of cells stretching from a central hall. In this way a small number of staff could ensure the easy supervision of the whole prison.

References can be found in many of the religious teachings which emphasise the need to treat people in a humane manner, even if they have committed crimes (**E**).

 D Sikh teaching

He who associates with evildoers is destroyed. Being fed on poison his life goes to waste.

Adi Granth 1343

 E Christian teaching

Remember those in prison as if you were their fellow prisoners, and those who are mistreated as if you yourselves were suffering.

Hebrews 13:3

stop and think!

- What, in your opinion, are the main reasons for sending a person to prison?

REFORM
JUSTICE
FORGIVENESS
REFORM
MERCY
REFORM
PUNISHMENT

All religions accept that, on occasions, punishment may have to be given to those who refuse to abide by society's rules. The aims of revenge and retaliation, however, have little place in their teachings. The key aims must centre on reform and protection, and the punishment must distinguish between the demands of justice and the need for forgiveness and mercy (**F**).

F The aims of punishment

QUESTIONS

1 What punishment would you regard as appropriate in the following cases?

a rape?

b football hooliganism?

c robbery with violence?

d causing death by reckless driving?

e kidnapping?

f blackmail?

g murder?

h vandalism?

i burglary?

j arson?

k not paying train fares?

l manslaughter?

2 When deciding on the punishment, what part do you think should be played by:

a justice?

b forgiveness?

c mercy?

d reform?

e retribution?

f reparation?

3 How do you think Christians should react to those in prison?

6 The ultimate punishment

A central principle of a just society is that every individual has a right to 'life, liberty and the pursuit of happiness'. It has been accepted for centuries that those individuals who violate this right must pay the ultimate penalty.

The debate about capital punishment for murder is dominated by two views. On the one hand, the murderers must be given the punishment which they deserve, which may be death. On the other hand, similar to the pacifist attitude to war, there is the view that under no circumstances is it possible to justify the use of the death penalty.

Arguments for capital punishment

- Society must protect civilians and those who fight crime from individuals who are unable to control their violent impulses.

- Friends and relatives of the victims have a right to expect retribution. In this way, justice is clearly seen to be 'done'.

- Too often, 'life' prisoners are released after a much shorter sentence and can be regarded as a great risk to the community.

- The death penalty is the only sort of deterrent that certain criminals will understand.

- Some criminals would much prefer to be executed than to spend the rest of their lives in prison. In 1977, in the USA, Gary Gilmore opted for death by firing squad rather than face a life sentence in prison. He felt that death was preferable.

stop and think!

- The sanctity of life does not apply in warfare or in some aspects of medical ethics, so why does it apply in punishment?

Arguments against capital punishment

- There have been **miscarriages of justice**: people have been executed for crimes they did not commit, (for example, Timothy Evans and Derek Bentley (see page 136).

- The death penalty does not seem to work as a deterrent: many murders are committed on the spur of the moment, or because of mental illness.

- Certain violent criminals and terrorists, if executed, could be seen as martyrs, and this might provoke extreme action.

- A civilised state must not be seen to violate the sanctity of life so blatantly.

- Some countries use the death penalty indiscriminately, to rid a government of its opponents.

- There is a certain lack of fairness seen in the judicial process: minority groups suffer most.

- Capital trials can be lengthy and very costly because of appeals. Juries are also less likely to convict if the death penalty is enforced.

Many countries throughout the world still have capital punishment. Despite the protests of groups such as Amnesty International many American states have the death penalty and others are considering re-introducing it.

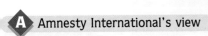

A Amnesty International's view

When the button is pressed, 2,400 volts surge into the body in a 2-minute burst. Doctors wait 10 minutes for the body to cool before examination. If still alive, another 2-minute burst is administered. The final cause of death is usually heart failure.

To make a person sit, day after day, night after night, waiting for the time when he will be led out of his cell to this death is cruel and barbaric… To be a mother or father and watch your child going through this living hell is a torment more painful than anyone can imagine.

stop and **think!**

Do you think that capital punishment has any place in a civilised society? Explain your answer.

B This horrific photo of an execution by electric chair of a woman was secretly taken by a witness during the 1920s. Public reaction led to several US States banning the death penalty.

The ultimate punishment

Until 1828 in Britain, death by hanging was the penalty for over 200 crimes, many of which would now be regarded as minor. People were hanged for trivial offences such as shooting a rabbit, picking pockets and even cutting down a tree in a park!

A number of well publicised cases in the 1950s led to the **abolition** of the death penalty in December 1969, although technically it could still be used in cases of **treason** or **piracy**.

Timothy Evans (**C**) was given a full **posthumous** pardon when it was proved that he did not murder his wife. Evans was slightly mentally retarded and easily influenced by Dr John Reginald Christie who was a lodger in his house. Not realising how serious a 'confession' would be, Evans informed the police that he had murdered his wife. He believed he would be in trouble with the police because he had allowed his wife to undergo an abortion (then illegal) at the hands of Christie. Christie acted as the chief witness against Evans but he, in turn, later confessed to the murders of seven women, including Mrs Evans, and was found guilty and hanged.

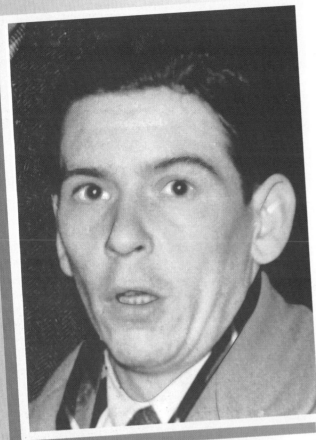

C Timothy Evans, just after his arrest

Derek Bentley (**D**) was hanged for the shooting of a policeman by his 16-year-old accomplice, Christopher Craig. Bentley was already under arrest and was being led away by police officers when Craig opened fire and killed a police officer. Despite this, and the fact that Bentley had a low mental age, he was executed because in the eyes of the law he was of adult age and was an accomplice to murder. The jury recommended mercy but, in spite of a petition to the Queen, he was executed, Craig escaped the death penalty by being under age. After a long campaign, Bentley was granted a limited posthumous pardon. His trial and conviction was seen as 'a **travesty** of justice' even by the standards of 1953.

D Derek Bentley, a few days before the shooting

Islam

In Islamic law, there are at least three crimes which carry the death penalty: murder, adultery and apostasy (abandoning your faith). It is vital that the question of guilt is clear before a sentence is carried out, and only the proper authorities can implement the law prescribed by the Shari'ah (**E**).

With accusations of adultery, at least four witnesses to the actual act must be provided: this will rarely be possible. If the accuser fails to prove their case, he or she can be severely punished for slander. A freely given confession repeated four times in court would be acceptable proof in place of the witnesses.

It should be remembered that in an Islamic state, Islam *is* the state, and therefore any act of apostasy which leads to open rebellion against Islam, is an act of treason. Even in Britain it is still possible, technically, to be executed for high treason.

stop and think!

> From 1931 to 1956 Albert Pierrepoint was Britain's official executioner. No one could be better placed to comment on the use of the death penalty.
>
> 'Executions are only an antiquated relic of a primitive desire for revenge which takes the easy way and hands over the responsibility for revenge to other people.'
>
> Alfred Pierrepoint, *The Independent*, 16 February 1991
>
> • What does Pierrepoint mean by 'the easy way'?
> • Would you ever send a mentally retarded person to prison?

Throughout all the teachings of the world religions there is an emphasis on the need for care to be taken when handing out punishment. Jesus pointed out to his followers how quick people are to criticise others while ignoring their own faults (**F**).

Similar sentiments can be found in the Qur'an (**G**).

Buddhists believe that punishment serves a purpose in protecting society from criminals but draws the line on harsh penalties, in particular, the death penalty. The teachings always emphasise the aim of reforming criminals (**H**).

 E Muslim teaching

Take not life, which Allah hath made sacred, except by way of justice and law.
Qur'an surah 6:151

 F Christian teaching

... Jesus said to them, 'If any one of you is without sin, let him be the first to throw a stone at her.'... Jesus straightened up and asked her, 'Woman, where are they? Has no one condemned you?'
'No one, sir,' she said.
'Then neither do I condemn you,' Jesus declared. 'Go now and leave your life of sin.'

John 8:7–11

 G Muslim teaching

If Allah were to punish men for their wrongdoing, He would not leave, on the earth, a single living creature.
Qur'an surah 16:61

 H Buddhist teaching

No matter how evilly someone behaves they always have the possibility of correcting their behaviour. To deny that possibility of change by imposing the death penalty, for example, is to contradict the whole spirit of Buddhism.
Human Rights from a Buddhist Perspective,
James Belither

QUESTIONS

1 Are the Christian and Buddhist viewpoints (**F** and **H**) realistic in this day and age?

2 'A man reaps what he sows.' (Galatians 6:7)

   a In what way does this quote appear to contradict the Christian teaching in **F**?

   b Which religious teachings are more in line with this saying?

3 '...The avenger of blood shall put the murderer to death when he meets him.' (Numbers 35:21) Why must we take care when we use such quotes to support a case for or against the death penalty?

1 Give four causes of war.

2 Which Christian denomination totally opposes participation in wa

3 What does the word 'jihad' literally mean?

4 What was the attitude of the early Christians towards war?

5 What are conscientious objectors?

6 Describe, explain and analyse:

a the differences between a holy war and a just war.

b Christian and Muslim attitudes to war and conflict.

7 Can you think of any problems which a country might face in attempting to meet all seven conditions for a just war?

a Do you think these conditions can be applied to a modern-day conflict?

b Could they be applied in the scenario of a nuclear war? Give reasons for your answer.

8 The Talmud states: 'If a person intends to kill you, be first to kill him'. The Qu'ran says, 'Fight in the way of Allah with those who fight you, but do not begin hostilities.' Is a defensive war therefore allowable?

9 Look at the cartoon below. What message is the cartoonist trying to give about modern-day warfare?

'It was going to be the ultimate weapon, but I can't lift it'.

10 The following poem, entitled 'The Dead', was written by Rupert Brooke, a British soldier who was killed in the First World War:

'These laid the world away; poured out the red
Sweet wine of youth; gave up the years to be
Of work and joy, and that unhoped serene,
That men called age; and those who would have been,
Their sons, they gave, their immortality.'

a What message is the poet trying to convey about the horror of war?

b Are you surprised that the poet, who was able to see so clearly the awful consequences of war, was also fighting in the war?

11 Outline the six main aims of punishment.

12 In England and Wales, criminal responsibility begins at the age of 10 years old. Is it right that children under this age cannot be prosecuted for criminal acts?

13 Can you think of any examples of killings that are regarded as legal or which, though illegal, would not be classed as murder?

14 What new teachings did Jesus add to those in the Old Testament about the law and the way the criminal should be treated?

15 How does Christianity try to maintain a balance between punishment and forgiveness when dealing with a criminal?

16 In Islamic law, murderers can be executed. However, the relatives of the victim can sometimes choose compensation from the killer rather than demand their death. A victim's family can at times be asked by a Muslim court to decide the murderer's fate by choosing between execution, compensation or freedom.

a Do you think it is a good idea to give the family of a victim the choice of punishment?

b Write down what you see as the advantages and disadvantages of such a system.

Points to remember

This book has been written to help you think about some of the major issues facing our world and how religious beliefs and teachings influence these issues. Whether you are using *One World: Many Issues* as part of a GCSE RE/PSE course or as part of a general RE/PSE course, we hope you find the book interesting and helpful. In writing this book there are four specific things we want you to remember.

- What you think is important and matters. We want to encourage you to think for yourself and to consider the different viewpoints and arguments which exist in the various issues you are studying.

- *One World: Many Issues* is about the place of religion in today's world, especially what differing religions have to say about contemporary problems and concerns. Whether you think religion is a force for good or bad in the world, there is no doubt it remains an important presence (if you disagree with this, then just watch the news for a week; it will be very surprising if religion does not feature).

- *One World: Many Issues* is designed to help you think about moral decisions and how we make moral choices (morals are often spoken of as making choices between right and wrong). When we make a moral choice (for example, finding some money in the street gives us a moral choice of: a) leaving the money, b) picking it up and keeping it, and c) picking it up and handing it in), there are all kinds of factors which influence our thinking. These include our conscience, our reasoning (thinking about the consequences of our actions), our family and friends. Within the world of religion there are other important factors, such as relevant teachings from sacred texts, tradition, and teachings from leaders of the religion today. Many of the major problems facing our world today were unknown at the time that some sacred texts were written. For example, the Bible does not directly speak about nuclear warfare or the ozone layer, but many Christians would say it does provide guidance on how we should care for our world and treat one another as human beings.

- Not everyone within an individual religion believes exactly the same things or practises their beliefs in the same way. This is especially true when thinking about religion and modern problems. If you asked a hundred Christians about their views on abortion, you would probably get a range of responses ranging from those who would say it could be right in certain circumstances, for example, if the pregnancy was caused by rape, to those who would say it could never be right. It is helpful to avoid phrases like 'all Jews believe that…' and it is important to recognise that there is diversity of belief, practice and viewpoints within the religions you are studying.

Ten examination tips

 1 Make sure that you understand the layout and structure of your exam paper and how many questions you have to do. Every year, there are some students who attempt every single question on the entire paper when they only had to do four questions. Doing too much means your answers will be rushed and will not have the depth you need.

2 Remember that your exam in RE, no matter how good your general knowledge, is about the issues your course has covered. You must know about the key beliefs, practices and teachings from the religions you have studied and how these can be applied to the issues you have discussed.

3 An important part of the examination is the evaluation element. This is where you have the opportunity to share your views and ideas on the issues you have studied. Often, students do badly in this part of the examination because they do not develop their ideas fully enough. For example, on capital punishment, a response might be that it is wrong because you can kill an innocent person. However, if that is the only reason given, it can only score 1 mark. The other main reason for students doing poorly is that they might only present points from one side of the argument. On euthanasia, for example, a student might produce several reasons why he or she is against it, but show no evidence of being aware of the reasons why some people are for it. The really good answer is where a student clearly supports his or her own view with a range of reasoned arguments, and also shows a good awareness of other people's points of view.

 4 Look carefully at how much each part of a question is worth. Avoid writing a long paragraph for a question worth only 1 or 2 marks but be aware that a question worth 10 marks will need a lot more than two or three sentences.

5 Make sure you know exactly how long you can spend on each question. If the exam is $1\frac{1}{2}$ hours and you have to do five questions, then that is eighteen minutes maximum per question. If you spend five minutes longer on the first four questions, you will have no time to answer the fifth question at all (so losing all the marks for that question).

6 If you have a choice of questions then exercise your choice carefully. Some students see the first part of a question, think they can answer it and rush into their response. They then realise they cannot do the other part of the question, and wish they had chosen another question. A few minutes careful reading before selecting your questions is vital.

 7 Have an effective revision plan and stick to it. With *One World: Many Issues* you might find it helpful to make your own notes at the end of each unit, so that you can recall these when you need to. Remember that you cannot recall what you have never learnt in the first place.

 8 Try to extend your reading. Magazines, newspapers, libraries and CD-ROMs all contain valuable information which can help you in your learning. Writing to organisations can greatly help you with coursework (but always enclose an SAE).

 9 Try to stay focused on your work. Examination times can be hectic and stressful, and it is unlikely that you will ever take so many exams again in such a short period of time! If you can sacrifice some of your social life for a while and commit yourself to your work, it will help you improve your performance.

 10 With coursework, be realistic about how much you can do. If you have been told an assignment should be about 1,000 words, then try to stick to this. Make sure your assignment allows you to use both your knowledge and understanding of the religions you have studied, and your own views and ideas.

Glossary

AAT 'Alpha-1-antitrypsin' – used to treat people with emphysema (lung disease) and cystic fibrosis

AIDS 'Acquired Immune Deficiency Syndrome' – a medical condition

Allah Muslim name for God in the Arabic language

abolition The enforced ending of something

agnostic An individual who believes that we cannot know for sure that God exists

annulment Roman Catholic declaration that a marriage bond never existed

arranged/assisted marriage The selection of marriage partners organised by the parents or relatives

atheist An individual who does not believe that God exists

banishment A punishment where offenders were sent abroad for a certain amount of time

battery farming Intensive breeding and rearing of animals

Buddha Title meaning 'awakened'; applied to Siddharta Gautama, the founder of Buddhism

calligraphy Beautiful writing; used as an art form, especially by Muslims

chador Muslim term for a large piece of cloth, worn by women to leave only the face exposed

chaos Total and utter confusion

chromosomes Structures that carry the inherited genetic information that influences the growth and functioning of the entire body

civil A legal marriage without a religious ceremony

conscience An inner feeling which tells us what is right and wrong

conscientious objector An individual who refuses to fight in a war because of his beliefs

contraception Methods used by couples to avoid pregnancy

destabilise Disrupt or upset

detrimental Harmful or damaging

diabetes A medical disorder caused by a lack of insulin

diminished responsibility Legal defence term used in murder cases meaning a person was not responsible for their actions

discrimination Prejudice in action – unfair treatment of an individual or group

DNA 'Deoxyribonucleic Acid' – carrier of all genetic information present in nearly all living organisms

Down's Syndrome Medical abnormality which leads to mental handicap and a characteristic physical appearance

dukkha First of the Four Noble Truths – Buddhist term relating to suffering

eternal Always existing; with no beginning and no end

ethics Moral principles; rules of conduct and behaviour

excommunicate Exclude or refuse to be allowed as a member of the Church

extinct No longer in existence

fertile Able to have children

free range Animals allowed to roam and graze freely

free will The ability to choose for ourselves whether to perform good or evil acts

fundamentalist Someone who holds extremely strictly to their beliefs

genetic engineering The process of changing the make up of living organisms

geometry Mathematical arrangement of objects or parts

gospel Literally means 'good news'
a. The name given to the first four books of the New Testament
b. Refers also to the Christian 'message' of salvation

Hebrew A community that was to become Israel

hijab Muslim term meaning modesty in dress

Humanist A non-religious person who believes in the importance of living life fully for the welfare of others

idolatry The worship of idols

incest Sexual intercourse between individuals who are too closely related to marry each other

infant mortality rate The number of children dying before reaching the age of one year

infidels People with no religious beliefs; in the past, a term used to describe any non-Christian

infinite Not limited in any way; endless

insulin Hormone that regulates the amount of glucose in the blood; an imbalance of it causes diabetes

karma Literally 'actions'. Law followed by Buddhists, Hindus and Sikhs; the results of one's actions determines the nature of future rebirth

manslaughter Legal term for the unlawful killing of a person – either unintended or where there is a reason which will be taken into account

martyr	Someone who dies for their faith or beliefs
miscarriage of justice	When someone has been unfairly accused and punished for a crime they did not commit
monogamy	The practice of being married to one person at a time
morality	Accepted rules and standards of behaviour
mourning	Expression of sorrow following the death of a person
murder	The illegal, deliberate killing of another person
nirvana	Buddhist term meaning state of secure, perfect peace
oestrogen	Hormone produced naturally in women, which, when taken daily in the contraceptive pill, prevents egg development
omnipotent	All powerful
omniscient	All knowing
Orthodox	a. Someone who accepts the established traditions of a particular religion b. Orthodox Church – one of the three main branches of the Christian Church
pagans	Those who do not belong to one of the main world religions
piracy	Robbery or highjacking of ships at sea
polygamy	The practice of having more than one husband or wife at the same time
population explosion	The sudden sharp increase in population in certain countries
pornography	The viewing/reading of explicit sexual matters
posthumous	Occurring after death
prejudice	'Pre-judging' a situation or a person; an unjustified dislike
progestogen	Reproductive hormone produced naturally in women, which, when taken daily in the contraceptive pill, prevents ovulation
Psalms	Book in the Old Testament containing sacred songs or hymns
qawwali	Religious poetry set to music, especially in Sufism
Reform	Jews who do not accept a number of the traditional observances of Orthodox Judaism
reconciliation	A reunion between parties in disagreement; settling of an argument

reincarnation	The belief in the rebirth of the spirit/soul in a new body
resurrection	The central Christian belief that Christ rose from the dead
sacred	Connected with religion or used for a religious purpose
sacrificial	Describing something valued that is given up for the sake of something else more important or worthy
secular	Not religious
Shari'ah	Islamic law – the 'way' of the Prophet
spiritual	Concerned and inspired by sacred or religious things
stereotype	An over-simplified or exaggerated picture of people or situations
steward	An individual appointed to keep order and look after another's property
stigma	A psychological mark, or sign of disgrace or discredit
Sufism	A Muslim mystical sect, differing in dress and customs
suicide	The intentional taking of one's own life
surrogacy	When one woman bears a child on behalf of another woman
theist	A believer in the existence of gods or a God
theory of evolution	The view, normally associated with the work of Charles Darwin, that the human race evolved developed from earlier, primitive forms of life
travesty	Something that is totally unfair or unjust
treason	Attempting to kill or overthrow the ruling body of a country
vagrancy	The state of having no place to live or regular work
vegan	An individual who refuses to eat or use any animal products
vegetarian	An individual who will not eat animal meat but may eat dairy products
Yemenite	Originating from the Republican of Yemen
Zakah	One of the Five Pillars of Islam – tax on income to provide money for the less fortunate